May O'Brien was born in 1932 and started work as a temporary clerk in the Irish Transport and General Workers' Union in 1947. In the 1960s she was only the second woman to be appointed as a full-time branch assistant. In 1982 she was appointed Woman's Affairs Official, the first such appointment in the trade union movement; in that role she set out to ensure that women members had a voice in decision-making within the union, in Congress, in their workplaces and in their life-time choices. In 1992 she retired but from time to time she conducts assertiveness training courses and is constantly surprised that women today still need the boost that these courses give.

MAY O'BRIEN

Clouds on My Windows

A DUBLIN MEMOIR

First published in Britain and Ireland in 2004 by
Brandon
an imprint of Mount Eagle Publications
Dingle, Co. Kerry, Ireland and
Unit 3, Olympia Trading Estate, Coburg Road, London N22 6TZ, England

2   4   6   8   10   9   7   5   3   1

ISBN 0 86322 335 4

The author and publisher gratefully acknowledge the support
of SIPTU in the publication of this book.

Cover design: Anú Design
Typesetting by Red Barn Publishing, Skeagh, Skibbereen
Printed in the UK

This book is dedicated to my parents, who owning so little gave us so much.

And to my brother, named Con in this book, whose premature death saddened us all.

The concept of writing this book was but a dream of mine and would have remained so were it not for the support and goodwill of my family. In particular my only sister, called Kate in this book, whose practical help and impetus made a dream become a reality.

My gratitude is unbounded to all who never doubted that I could do it, and to whom I also dedicate this book.

CHAPTER ONE

T HE FIRST DAY I saw the old Liberty Hall as a workplace, I was terribly disappointed. It looked so down at heel and dark as it sat there brooding alongside the Liffey.

It was in 1947. I was fifteen years old and about to start my first job. After national school I had been awarded a Dublin Corporation grant to do a commercial course at Technical School, and now I was about to become a temporary clerical worker at the Irish Transport and General Workers' Union, paid thirty shillings per week for a five-and-a-half-day week—riches beyond my wildest dreams.

Without the commercial course, I would probably, at fourteen, have joined my friends who went working in sewing factories, shops or hospitals. But as I approached the gloomy old Liberty Hall that morning, I envied the girls going to work in some well-lit, noisy factory with plenty of things happening from the minute they stepped in the door.

This building had been a hotel, and I knew the British had shelled it in 1916. As I looked at it from Butt Bridge that sunny morning, it didn't look as though they'd done an awful lot of repairs since. The railings leaned sideways and needed a coat of paint. There were blank-looking windows, one broken, and with its peeling paint it looked as though its good times were long gone.

I went up the granite steps and in the big open doorway. I paused in the darkness. Should I knock or call out? Close by me a door creaked open and a little man stood there. There was something eerie about the way he had suddenly appeared like a genie out of a bottle.

"Whatchawant?" he grunted, anything but pleased to see me.

Silently I offered him my letter. He turned and disappeared, the door creaked closed, and another door nearer to me opened, and there he was again.

"Ye're in the wrong place," I thought he said.

As he spoke his body went into some kind of convulsion, his head twisted to one side, and his words seemed to be strangled at birth. I waited, appalled, not knowing what to do. I will never forget the sound he made. It was almost as though a devil had taken over his body. He then moved forward, took my arm and pushed me towards the top of the granite steps. He stopped, tried to speak again and couldn't.

I waited, not knowing what I should do. He was such a small man that I towered over him. He was wearing a greasy cloth cap, a scruffy khaki shirt and a scarf tied tightly around his scrawny neck, with dark blue dungarees and a jacket that was miles too big. His walnut wrinkled face was contorted, his black buttony eyes screwed up, and spittle came from lips that seemed to have a life of their own.

"Down there, beyond the shop, the brown door," he said through the spittle that covered his mouth.

"Thanks, mister," I muttered, and hurried away in the direction he indicated. When I looked back he was still standing at the corner, his body twitching, his head tilted to one side and, I suppose, those awful sounds still coming from him.

Inside the brown door I paused to pull myself together. It was a hallway with a steep wooden staircase, uncovered and none too clean. The litter from the bus stop outside had found its way in and waited to be picked up. At the top of the stairs there was a door marked Theatre and Cinema Branch, with an unmarked door beside it. I was looking for the Clothing Branch, so I pushed in the unmarked door. It led to a long, empty, high-ceilinged room with a wooden floor and two almost full-length windows, both dirt-encrusted. A metal dust-bin stood on two cement blocks, and beside it stood a wooden garden shed with its door heavily padlocked. I paused, wondering what on earth that was doing there.

Suddenly the door at the other end of the room opened and a man stood outlined. He was an elderly man with wire-framed glasses, his hair scarce on top, and he was buttoning his overcoat with one hand and holding a briefcase and newspaper in the other.

"Well, and who do we have here?" he asked. "Oh, it's the new recruit come to do the books, isn't that right?"

I smiled and handed him my letter. He read it quickly, and then handed it back to me.

"Come in, come in," he said, bringing me into the office and taking my coat to hang on a coat rack. "I'm Jim Gilhooley, your branch secretary. What's your name again?"

"May O'Brien," I told him, and we shook hands. He cleared a space at a table and told me to sit down and relax, then paused, obviously at a loss.

"I'm on my way out to a meeting. I can't stay, I'm afraid, even though it's your first day. Now what can we give you to do? Let's see. Oh yes, sure, Sadie will know. She'll set you right." He went to the door and called her name. He smiled at me. "You'll be all right then. See you later." And then he was gone.

A woman came in and looked at me appraisingly. She was elderly, pale faced, and wearing nondescript, kind of woolly clothes.

"You're the new young one," she said, with something of a sniff. "Well, you're punctual, I'll give you that. Sit down there," she said.

I looked around me with interest. It wasn't at all as I had expected an office to be. It was just a room with a big table littered with stuff and about twenty chairs with their backs to the walls.

"Now, let's see what we can start you with," she said. She shuffled around the piles of stuff on the table and drew something out. She picked up an enormous leather-bound book and placed it before me on the table. I looked at it with awe. It was the biggest book I'd ever seen. She then took up a smaller book with a mottled cover and opened it.

"Our members pay threepence or fourpence each week as union contributions. What they pay is entered into this book," she said, pointing to the mottled-covered book. "The payments are transferred into this register, where it can easily be read. The union number is that one there," pointing to handwritten numbers in the mottled book, with amounts of money beside it.

"That printed number in the register is the union number there. Do you see it?" I nodded. "Now, what you'll do is transfer that amount from that book into that register in the right week. You see the date at the top?" I nodded again. "You write each payment from that into the register, remembering always that the union number is the key. Then neatly tick off the item as you post it into the register. It must be neat and tidy, with no blots and no scrub-outs. If you can't find a number, leave it, and we'll go back over it later. Do you understand?"

Numbly I nodded, pen in hand, and off she went. To reach the top of the register I had to stand up and lean over the big book. There were little boxes in the register, and I could see the line of four pences down the page for the last week that been entered. I looked at the mottled book, checked I had the right date and that the member's number corresponded, then entered my first fourpence in the register, looking at it with the pride of a craftsman. Then I looked at the size of the register and the pile of sheets to be transferred. "Oh God! This will take for ever!"

I went on transferring the money from the book to the register, feeling that my figures were like little soldiers with their guns all facing the same way. In the adjoining room I could hear raised voices, telephones ringing, doors opening and closing, but in my sanctum there was only the squeak of my pen and the crackle of the open fire. My lines of little soldiers began to look a little less like a parade-ground army, their ranks went a little off line, and their guns wavered a bit as my eyelids grew heavy in the sweltering heat of the fire.

Suddenly outside my room there was a commotion. The voices were raised ever higher; doors thumped open and then slammed shut. There was the sound of swearing and the thud of angry feet approaching nearer and nearer. My door burst open and the enraged face of a man appeared around it. "Did ye see Terry? The little bastard! I swear I'll tear him limb from limb when I get hold of his scrawny neck!" I sat petrified with fear. The man came into the room, and I could feel his white-hot anger radiating out from him.

"Oh, you're new," he said, his voice straining to be polite. "I'm Tommy McCarthy. I work next door in the Building Branch. What's your name?" I muttered my name and he offered me his hand. I shook it, wincing at the pressure. "If you see that little bastard, that little runt, will you tell him I'm looking for him and that I'll kill him when I get him!"

"I don't know. . ."

"He's a little dwarf with a weasel's face. Once seen never forgotten." Then he smiled. "I'm only joking. Do you want a cup of tea?" With that he was gone, and I could hear his voice receding into the distance.

"Terry, Terry, you little bastard! Where the hell are you?"

I went back to my army of figures, wondering what on earth kind of place this was and why the man was so angry. After a while the door opened again, and a different man came in with a mug of tea in one hand and a bag of sugar in the other. He balanced a saucer over the mug with a few biscuits on it.

"There y'are. The Bull said you needed tea and tea you've got. My name is Paddy McLaughlin, and I work with that ignorant bull of a man. What's your name?" Again I muttered my name. He put everything down in a space he made by shoving things out of his way with his elbow. We then shook hands. Again I winced. These men had no idea of the strength and power of their hands. He poked the fire vigorously, and then stood with his back to it, legs apart, warming himself.

"You're being a bit neglected, aren't you? D'you know why?"

I shook my head and ventured a sip of the tea. It tasted like tar. It stuck in my throat and wouldn't go down. Hurriedly I took a bite of a biscuit, hoping that this would clear it.

"Sugar?" he asked affably.

I shook my head. "No, thanks."

"I thought all you young ones had a sweet tooth. I brought it in especially for you. We use condensed milk ourselves, the sweetened stuff, you know. Ah well." He helped himself to a biscuit. "So, why the neglect? Well, there's a strike looming ahead for Jumbo. That's your branch secretary. There's a five o'clock deadline today. If no offer comes before that, then the factories will stop working at eight o'clock tomorrow morning, and the shit will really hit the fan, if you'll pardon my French. So there's a conclave on next door with the bigwigs, and Jumbo is gone to a meeting with the employers' association. He'll come back carrying his shield or lying on it." He laughed, but I saw nothing funny.

"Mr McCarthy was shouting for Terry and saying. . ." I paused, not sure how to say it.

Paddy teetered on his heels before the fire, his hands in his trousers pockets. He laughed. "You mean he's wanting to tear him limb from limb? Ah, but that's par for the course. Terry has an allergy. . ."

"Is he the man with the stammer?" I asked. "It really is awful. I never. . ."

"Terry? M'm. Yes, it's supposed to have been caused by the British soldiers, you know. There was a raid for guns and Terry wouldn't talk. They left him like that."

"And he has an allergy too?" I asked.

"Yes," Paddy chuckled. "Terry is allergic to one thing only and that's work. When he sniffs it in the breeze he's gone like a flash. He's like a fox, boltholes all over the place. When Tommy McCarthy is looking for him, he'll stay under cover for hours. You see, Tommy wants him to make ballot boxes. Terry's averse to doing all that labour in the one day. He knows if he stays out of reach they'll be made by some of the boys. They're handy with their hands, you see."

He moved to the door and paused halfway through.

"The toilet's through that door over there," he said. "The key's that one there on the mantelpiece." With a nod and a wink he was gone.

I couldn't drink the tea but gratefully ate the biscuits. I then ventured to the toilet and washed the mug and the bent spoon that had been part of the service. When I came back, the place was buzzing with people. Jim Gilhooley was talking to them about what had happened at his meeting. When he saw me, he called out over the noise, "You can go to your lunch now. D'you need a few bob?" He put his hand into his pocket.

"It's all right, thanks. I'm OK," I responded gratefully and went off.

Outside I checked my little purse. My mother had given me a half-crown that morning as she stood at the door to see me off. "Make sure you get something to eat," she'd reminded me. "Something decent and filling, not chocolate or stuff like that. And don't forget, it's a long way off to pay day."

I'd be paid on Friday, thirty whole shillings, wealth indeed! But I knew all too well that there was no way the family purse would run to a half-crown a day for me between now and Friday, so I would have to be thrifty.

Chips? Yes, there was a chipper just around the corner in Marlboro Street. Would I get a few sweets for the kids? But I had to make sure to keep my bus fare, and that would make a big hole in my purse. Could I walk to work? It was a bit far from our council house in Donnybrook, but maybe I could walk home. Could I get a bike? I felt really grown-up making these kinds of decisions for myself with nobody leaning over my shoulder saying, "Do this or do that."

When I got back the meeting was still going on, but there was a more relaxed air about the place. Apparently they were waiting for Jim Gilhooley to return to confirm something with the company, or so I gathered. I went back to my army of figures and worked away, enjoying filling in the blank spaces.

"You've let the fire go out," Jim Gilhooley said accusingly.

I looked up at him in total shock. He was back from his meeting and hanging his coat on the coat rack. I realised then that the room was quite cold and the fire was indeed almost out. I also realised he was extremely angry.

"What. . .?"

"Did nobody tell you about the fire? I suppose they didn't."
He started to poke out the guts of the fire.

"I didn't know. . ." I started stupidly.

"Take that key and go out to the coal shed and get a few sticks.
Fill that bucket with coal, and I'll do what I can here."

He took the inside pages of his newspaper, holding them in
front of the fire to make a draught. I picked up the bucket, the
shovel and the key and hurried outside. The padlock on the garden shed door was hard to undo, and when I got it open it was
pitch dark inside. Trying to forget about lurking spiders, I
grabbed some sticks and shovelled coal into the bucket, re-locked
the door and struggled to carry the full bucket back to the office.

"Ah, good girl. That's the ticket. She's pulling well now."

He took the newspaper down and fed sticks and then coal
around the little pyramid he'd built and watched with satisfaction as the flames licked into them. He stood up, brushed his
trousers legs and refolded what was left of his paper.

"I'm sorry," I stuttered.

"You didn't know, girl," he said, wiping his hands on a wad of
newspaper. "You see, this place is reeking with damp. It's only
the fires that keep it at bay. I'm bronchial. Pneumonia is the
danger. Once you've inhaled coal dust, you're never the same.
You see, I'm from Arigna." I hadn't a clue what he meant.

He looked at his still-dirty hands. "We both need a wash. I'll
go first. Don't touch anything in the meantime, mind."

Off he went and I stood in front of the fire crestfallen. My
hands were black, and when I looked at my face in the mirror, I
had streaks of black on the end of my nose and my chin. I did
the best I could with the cold water, noting that the clean white
blouse that I'd ironed so carefully that morning was decidedly
grubby about the cuffs and collar.

At six o'clock I was told I could go home, and as I queued at the bus stop I was aware that some terrible crisis in the office had been averted, but I didn't really know what, or why that should be so.

I knew that I must never, ever, let the fires go out. That seemed to be the most heinous crime of all. I was obviously destined to visit that garden shed again and again with all its scariness and the enormous spiders that I knew lurked there just waiting for me. I got home full of my day's news, only to find that one of my brothers was sick and he might have to go to hospital. In the face of such anxiety, all I could do when asked how the day had gone was to say, "Fine!" and leave it at that.

CHAPTER TWO

I SAT IN the bus next morning knowing I'd be early for work. It had been a difficult night. My youngest brother had a high fever. My mother and father had stayed up and tried to ease his discomfort. The doctor had called and, with much head shaking, had given an antibiotic. He had been grave and concerned. Echoes of the past, I'm sure, lingered with my parents. They'd buried their first-born at the age of six and obviously feared a second loss.

The doctor's return visit this morning would tell the tale. If the fever didn't abate, my brother would be taken into hospital. That was a scenario nobody wanted to discuss. My father had opted to go to work but to come back for the doctor's visit. Since he wouldn't be paid for the time he was off and extra money would be needed for medical things, that was quite significant. To talk to my mother about bus fares was impossible in that situation. Checking again what was left in my purse, I was a bit anxious. This was only Tuesday, but my funds were dwindling rapidly, and I had to last out to Friday! I'd started off with a few pence of my own money in my purse as well as the half-crown, and I knew I had five shillings and sixpence in the post office, but that was meant to go towards buying me new shoes. The ones I had on had a cardboard cut-out to cover the hole in the sole.

As I sat on the bus, I thought about the first job I ever had. God, that job had been awful! One of the nuns had arranged it with my mother. "Sure, she might as well be occupied during the holidays," the nun had said, "and earning a few bob in a nice atmosphere." The job had been as a teacher's aide in a private school. I suppose I'd been a glorified sort of babysitter really, but I'd loved being with the children. There was one English class for eight-year-olds that the teachers all hated because the kids would act up out of boredom. However, I had found the kids loved role-playing stories, particularly the bloodthirsty bits, and would hang on after the bell to finish out the scene. That didn't make me exactly popular.

However, my real problem was the common room between classes. It was like living in a petrified forest where everything was set in stone. I was so out of place that I was made to feel a freak. There were feuds between individuals, chairs that could only be sat in by so-and-so, teachers who wouldn't eat if another teacher was in the room. And the backbiting! Oh God! I'd been glad when that school broke up and my job there ended.

When I got to the brown door on Eden Quay, the cleaner opened it for me on her way out. She was a thin little driven-looking woman with an enormous bag, which seemed to weigh a ton.

"There ye are," she greeted me. "It's yourself, the new young one. God love you, you poor kid. It's a madhouse in there and the dirt! Sure, you couldn't get this place clean." She looked down her nose disapprovingly at the cigarette packets and sweet papers already beginning to accumulate in the hallway.

"You'd never think that I mopped that out only a half-hour ago."

She went off with a sniff, and I resumed my place in the office at the corner of the table. What the cleaner said was true, this place would be impossible to keep clean. Admittedly, the brown lino on the floor was so polished you could nearly see your face in it and the fireplace was spic-and-span and the fire drawing nicely. The tops of things had been dusted and the bits of table that were exposed had been polished. The walls, cream on top and chocolate brown at the bottom, seemed to exude dust from their pores, dust you could see in the sunlight that somehow got in. The wall space was filled by chairs, backs to the wall and evenly spaced. Today each chair had an accumulation of papers, boxes and things, set out in some sort of order. They hadn't been there yesterday. I wondered. . .

In a corner two flags were folded. One was the Tricolour contained in a sort of case. You could see the green, white and orange peeping through. The other was a dark blue flag with a fringed border of gold, and scattered on it were silvery stars. It was folded more haphazardly. Big poles meant to hold up the flags were telescoped to fit into the confined space. I wondered what the blue flag represented.

On the walls were pictures of men making speeches, mainly to men, and men marching with placards led by the Tricolour and that odd blue flag. Men at meetings in serried ranks with a few women merged into the background. Men with old-fashioned guns. What were they doing?

There was one picture of a woman on her own, and she looked very different. She was beautiful in a long-ago kind of way. She was dressed in a sort of ball-gown. That was odd. There was an enormous glass-fronted bookcase against the wall beside the fireplace. I looked at the books; they were all tattered, dull, and looked as though they had never been read.

Outside in the back lane lorries came, unloaded and went away to good-natured banter amongst the men. I opened my register again and looked through it. The members were set apart in factories, men together paying fourpence, and the women, many more, paying threepence.

Their ages, addresses and dates of entry into the union were written in. Some of the names of the factories I recognised: Cassidy's, Burton's, TJ Cullen's and Bradmola out in Blackrock. Girls I knew worked in some of these places, and they were paid a minimum rate but depended for real earnings on how much work they each produced. I'd heard only too often about girls working to breaking point to earn that money. Not only for the sake of the money itself, scarce though that would be, but so that they wouldn't be hounded by a narky supervisor standing behind their backs all day.

I looked at the page at the point where I'd left off the day before and surveyed my army of figures marching down the page. It might be boring, but it was infinitely better than working with some jumped-up Johnnie breathing down my neck to try to make me go faster. I took up my payments sheets, and again my army marched down the page.

Sadie bustled in. "So you're an early bird, that's good. And working away, that's good too. Things were a bit of a shambles yesterday. I hadn't had time to bless myself."

She checked the stuff on the chairs and then continued. "Jim wore himself out yesterday trying to solve that dispute in Burton's. Unofficial strikes are dreadful. It's amazing how those little gurriers, who wouldn't raise their voices above a whisper, suddenly think they're James Connolly leading a workers' revolution. Anyway, the position now is that we have had an offer to put to the members, so we'll all be gone for much of the day."

She looked at me a bit doubtfully. "So you'll be on your own. Do you think you can manage?"

I shared her doubts.

"You see, we have to meet the cutters, put the offer to a ballot, then count the votes and report back. We have to try not to have the thing escalate. Ah well, you can only do the best you can."

She started to put the papers from the chairs into boxes, and some men arrived to help with the chore. Then they carried the boxes down to street level where there was apparently a car waiting.

Sadie took me aside. "Now, you'll be here on your own. I'll show you what to do. Come here."

We went out into the bigger room. "The members stay that side of the counter, you stay that side. Do you understand?"

A wooden counter ran down the room from inside the door for about three yards at waist level. Inside there were rough wooden presses with doors with little latches. There was a big desk laden with stuff right in front of the fireplace. The fireplace itself was bigger and more ornate than the one in the room I'd been in and the fire was a mass of red coals. There was a telephone on the desk with an extension box. She pointed to it.

"If it rings, just say the officials are at a meeting and they will be back later. Get the person's name, and take a message if need be."

She took a brand-new jotter out of a drawer and said, "Put the messages here, and always get the name. Write down the time of the call too, and be polite even if they're not. Now, will you be all right?"

She got one of the men to bring in my work from the other room, and soon my register was balanced precariously on the desk and my pen poised to start my army on the move again.

Jim Gilhooley came bustling in. "Come on! Come on! We should've been on the job earlier. Now, are we right? Ballot papers, 'For' and 'Against'. Ballot boxes, one for each end of the canteen, and list of members. Are they all paid up, Sadie?"

She nodded. I wondered how she could know since the payments I was posting were backdated a number of weeks, but it was only a passing thought. . .

"Joe and Ollie, you'll act as checkers at the boxes. Make sure there's no messing. Nobody votes unless they're entitled to. We'll get some of the members to sit in for the count. All right?"

The men weren't as serious as the union people. They leaned on the counter, smoked cigarettes and laughed at each other's quips, going off in the end a bit reluctantly, I thought.

Jim was last out, and he turned to me just before he closed the door. He pointed to a key ring on the mantelpiece.

"That's the key to lock up the place at lunchtime. We'll be back before six o'clock. Make yourself a cup of tea. The stuff is in that press there." He pointed and I nodded. "And what must you remember above all else?"

"Keep the fires going," I responded with a grin.

"Exactly! And if you've any problems, the lads next door will help you out. Is that all right?"

"Yes, Mr Gilhooley, I'll do the best I can."

"I don't believe in titles," he said with a smile. "I am Jim; that's the way I prefer it."

I was now alone and monarch of all that I surveyed. This was only my second day in the job, and I'd been trusted to look after the whole show. I sat back and looked around me with a proprietorial air. When my eye lit on the telephone I stopped. I'd made about three phone calls in my whole life. In my limited experience, phone calls were almost invariably "bad news", officialdom of some kind. Now if that phone rang, I'd have to answer it and make sense out of whoever was on the other end.

I swallowed the lump in my throat. What would I say? Well, I suppose the name of the place for a start. I opened the first page of the brand-new jotter and wrote carefully: "Hullo, this is the

Irish Transport and General Workers' Union, Clothing Branch. How may I help you?"

God! It was a terrible mouthful, but when I tried it out, feeling a perfect fool, it sounded all right. I looked into the presses. There were envelopes, carbon paper and receipt books, more of the mottled-cover books I had before me, then the tea things in a press to themselves. There were cups and saucers, plates, jug and sugar bowl, teapot and a very black and battered kettle, tea, sugar, biscuits. But there was no milk. I could get the water from the tap in the toilet, and I could get milk in the shop downstairs, but how to boil the kettle?

I thought about my problem, how to boil the kettle. The fire? There was a tripod kind of thing lying on the hearthstone. It might slide over the metal of the fire grate and hold the kettle. I tried, and after several failures I got it latched on the metal grate. I filled the kettle, then took the key and my purse with my precious few coins and locked the door behind me, remembering to take the receiver off the telephone in case a call came while I was out. Now I would go to get the milk down in the shop.

The shop was a busy newsagent and tobacconist, selling bits of everything. There were a number of men in the shop, though they didn't seem to be buying anything. There were two shop assistants, both women. The little wispy one was unpacking stuff to put up on the shelves and having an argument with some of the men. The plump smiley woman came forward.

"What can I get you?" she asked.

"Half pint of milk, please." I put the exact amount of coins on the counter. She handed the milk to me and put the money in the till.

"Do you work for Jim Gilhooley? They said there was a new young one coming."

I nodded.

"First day?" one of the men asked.

"Second," I responded shortly, wondering why on earth he'd be interested. There were a few quips thrown which I didn't understand and I turned to go.

"If you want, you can get your stuff on tick," the woman said with a smile. "You don't have to pay on the nail. It's a long way to Friday. That's your first pay day, I suppose?"

I nodded, knowing my mother's reaction would be to say, "What we can't pay for we can't afford."

"Remember, you don't need to be without," the woman said, with a smile. "Just say the word."

The other woman intervened. "Nellie, there's that cheese sandwich lying there. . ."

"Oh yes! It's ready for Peter Joyce and he won't be in. His wife is ill. D'ye want it? It'll go to waste otherwise."

One of the men said something about him never being offered anything free, and the little woman said not to mind him, he got too much of everything free. That led to a heated argument, mainly about politics, I think. The sandwich was in a bag and in my hand before I knew where I was. As I left there was a chorus of "Good luck" and "Take it easy" from the men.

As I returned to the office I wondered about the shop. It seemed odd that they knew so much about the office and what went on there. The little woman had really wanted me to have that sandwich as well as the milk, and all that stuff about things on tick. I didn't know what to make of it.

I put the kettle on the tripod thing, put out my plate with its sandwich, a cup and saucer, my bottle of milk and a few biscuits on a tray, and spooned the tea into the teapot. I felt like a child playing house. Then just as the kettle was steaming the phone rang.

I sat transfixed for a moment with shock. Then I removed the kettle from the fire, put my message pad in place and intoned my mantra into the receiver.

"Who's that?" a male voice asked.

"The officials are at a meeting and will be back around six o'clock," I intoned, keeping strictly to the script.

"This is Eddie," the voice said, "but who you?"

"Do you want to leave a message?" I asked in my best voice.

"Are you blonde or brunette?" the voice asked.

"Why? What on earth has that got to do with it?"

"I just. . .Oh, it's the new kid. Jim said there was a young one coming. Sure, it's only a bit of fun. You can say it's Eddie, I'm chair of the branch, and I just want to know what's happening. People ask me, you see, and I'm supposed to know. Ask him to ring me."

"OK. Eddie the chair rang. Ring him. That's the message. All right?"

"Exactly," he chuckled. "That's it in a nutshell." He rang off laughing.

Almost immediately the phone rang again with almost exactly the same performance, and it rang six times after that in quick succession, with different people asking much the same question. As I put the phone down the sixth time and began to write the message in the jotter, a man came in and leaned on the counter, spreading his newspaper on it to read it. He was stocky, grey-haired, wore dark-framed glasses, and he had a very cross look about him.

"You've let the fire go out," he remarked, eyes still on his paper.

"I have not," I retorted indignantly, checking the fire behind me.

"The one inside. Jim's fire. He'll be very mad."

Shock made me weak at the knees. "God, no. It couldn't. . ." I remembered I'd not checked it since they'd all left. "Oh, my God!" It was the one thing I was not to forget. I ran in and he was right. I stood, hand to my mouth in dismay, and looked at it.

"No use going into mourning. There's work to be done," the man said. He took off his jacket, placed it on the back of a chair, rolled up his shirtsleeves and began to tear pieces off his newspaper. "Get sticks, and there's more paper out there, and bring in the lid of the dustbin."

I looked at him in surprise.

"For the ashes, of course," he said. He started to rake out the fire, putting the cinders to one side and then the ashes on to the bin lid. "There's a container in the bin for the ashes." I took them out and disposed of them as he indicated. When I got back he'd lit the fire again, and the flames were beginning to catch the coals. He swept up the hearthstone and looked at his work with pride, then stood up. "That should do it!"

"I can't believe it!" I was nearly crying.

He wiped his hands on a bit of rag, rolled down his sleeves and put on his jacket, straightening his tie in his reflection in the bookcase.

"Fires need to be looked at every half hour when they're going well, more often when they're not. Like little children. . . You can't leave them on their own. You see, I did the trans-Atlantic crossing as a ship's stoker, so I do know a bit about fires."

He smiled and extended his hand. "I'm Frank Robbins, branch secretary of the Theatre and Cinema Branch. That's the first door at the top of the stairs."

I told him my name and we shook hands.

"I'm very grateful," I stammered. "The phone kept ringing. . ."

"And you kept answering. I know. . . But you've got to set your priorities, and the fires are high on the list in this branch. Now, it's well past your lunch hour. So disconnect the phone, lock the door and take your break. You don't have to go back on duty till half-two. All right?"

He started to fold the remnants of his newspaper into his pocket, turning to the door. I tried again to thank him.

"That's between us. It need go no further," he said, pausing in the doorway. "How old are you, as a matter of interest?"

"Fifteen."

"And we've the gall to call ourselves socialists!" he snorted, and closed the door behind him.

CHAPTER THREE

I DID AS he advised. The tea helped, the sandwich even more so, but all through my meal I went over and over the scenario. How on earth could I have been such a fool? To let two fires go out in two days? It was beyond belief.

When I was finished I washed up the tea things, put the stuff tidily away in the presses and dusted away my crumbs. By 2.29 p.m. on the clock on the mantelpiece, I had the door unlocked, the phone back on the receiver, checked my fires were all right and was ready for business. I had another three phone calls about Burton's, one a snooty woman's voice demanding to speak to Jim Gilhooley. When I asked her name she was utterly shocked.

"This is head office," she responded.

"Who's calling from head office?" I asked. A reasonable question in my view since I didn't know what "head office" meant.

"The general president," she answered, a little faintly.

"Who?"

A man's voice with a Belfast accent then came on. "Billy McMullen here. Who's that?"

"This is May O'Brien," I said. "I started yesterday."

"Oh, the new recruit. All right. Well, the Press has been on about a strike in Burton's. Do you know anything about that?"

"There's a vote today. That's all I know. Can I ask Jim to ring you?"

"Do that."

Two visitors then arrived. The first was a young man in his early twenties. He was small and dark, and he leaned on the counter, drumming his knuckles impatiently on the wood as I wrote down the details of the recent conversation.

"I've been sacked," he said. "I'm a presser up in Fisher's. The oily little bastard sacked me when I went in this morning, and when I went back after the lunch break he wouldn't let me on to the premises. My stuff's still there. The rotten, cross-eyed little git!"

I didn't know how to write that down, but somehow I would have to get the facts of the story.

"How long have you worked there?"

"Nine weeks."

"Any complaints about your work?"

"Nothing about my work. It's up with the best. Anybody would tell you that. Just 'cause I'd a few jars at the weekend, and with the ould head on Monday, sure I just couldn't go in. It was dog rough."

"Has it happened before?"

"Hold on there! Who do you think you are? Of course it's happened before. I enjoy me ould pint. Nothing wrong in that!"

"I've the message written down, and I'll give it to the first official I see, and I'll say it's urgent. That's all I can do."

"You just tell the union man it's Joe Lynch, the presser. He knows me, and I want a bit of action from him. I pay me union dues and I want a bit of service. You can tell him that too."

When he went I tore the page out of the jotter and started the message again. I wrote:

"Joe Lynch, presser in Fisher's for nine weeks. Sacked this

morning for absence on Monday due to hangover. Wants imme-
diate action."

The other visitor was an old man. He came in puffing and
panting after his climb up the stairs. I was caught in a dilemma.
I'd been told members outside the counter, staff inside. All the
chairs were inside, yet I felt I should offer the man a chair while
he recovered. He was gasping and spluttering as he leaned on
the counter for support. I got a chair and pushed it to him outside the counter.

"Maybe you'd like a sit-down for a minute. Those stairs are
steep. I'm sorry I can't ask you to sit by the fire, but I'm only new,
and I've been told staff inside this counter, members outside. I
don't know why."

He sat down, more in surprise than anything else, I think.
"Thanks. You're very kind."

He began to breathe a little more evenly. "I'm Ned Carey.
And you are, my dear. . .?"

I told him my name and he stood and shook my hand, then
seated himself again. "What can I do for you?" I asked, leaning
over the counter towards him.

"Well, I wanted to see Jim. A little matter of business, you
might say. You see, I'm a master tailor and I'm making him a
suit, for a family wedding, I understand. I've done the measures.
I've got a nice bit of material picked out, so all I need to know
is his preference. You know, the style of the suit. Single-breasted,
DB, what type of lapel he wants: that kind of thing. The style, in
other words."

He heaved himself to his feet. "Would you tell him, my dear
girl, that I'd be obliged if he'd call to see me?" He shook my hand
again, murmuring something about it being a pleasure to have
made my acquaintance, and then moved off to face the stairs
again. I thought about how to write that message down. I knew

well that the way I took messages would be a test. This seemed a rather personal thing and I wanted it to be right. So I wrote:

"Ned Carey—master tailor—re details for your new suit. Please call to see him."

Jim Gilhooley arrived back in the office at about five o'clock looking tired and out of sorts.

"Any messages?" he asked, throwing off his coat. I noticed it was wet. It must be raining outside. It was strange not to have known, but I'd been inside here all day, bar the visit to the shop.

"Yes, I wrote them all down in this," I said, handing him the jotter. "Would you like a cup of tea?"

"It'd save my life," he said with a laugh. "It was rough going in Burton's. We solved one problem and caused another." He was glancing through the pages of my jotter as he spoke, and I could see a bit of a smile hovering about his mouth.

"You've been a busy girl, haven't you? You have a certain clarity of expression in your note-taking." He went off into his office chuckling to himself, and I busied myself getting the tea ready. When I brought it in to him on a tray, he was sitting in front of the fire warming his hands, and he looked cold and miserable.

"That message from head office," he said. "Who exactly were you talking to?"

"Billy McMullen, he said his name was. Haven't I spelt it right?"

He turned the jotter so that I could read my message.

"3.21 p.m. Head office, Billy McMullen, general president. Query from Press re Burton's. Please ring."

"Is that the right way?" I asked, beginning to doubt myself. "I mean I've never. . ."

"Excellent," he smiled. "Succinct and to the point."

I didn't know exactly what that meant, but it seemed that it was all right. I turned to go.

"The cutters stopped work for more money," he said. "They wanted a more realistic bonus system. We got it for them, and they voted three to one for the deal today. Now the pressers and the machinists want to be paid for the money they lost because no work was coming through from the cutters to them. They'll be down to basic wages, and the company says, 'No way.' They can't justify paying workers for work they haven't done."

"But it's not their fault," I said.

"Exactly. But how do we resolve it? If the rest of the factory stops tomorrow, the boss man is just going to say, 'I'm turning the key in the lock,' and he would walk away. That would mean that almost 300 people would lose their jobs."

He paused, cradling the cup of tea in his hands.

"You've done well holding the fort on your own. So why don't you go off home now. It's good to take a little time off now and again."

Obviously he wanted time on his own to consider how he'd deal with his problem, and I didn't envy him his thoughts.

I nodded, said, "Thanks" and "Goodnight," cleared the stuff from my desk and went off, head down, into the rain.

As the bus came nearer to home, the dread that I had kept at the back of my mind all day surfaced like a spectre. Any ill child is so helpless, so vulnerable, their hold on life is so fragile, and when it's one of your own family! When I got off the bus, I ran home as quickly as I could, wondering what the news would be.

CHAPTER FOUR

WHEN I GOT to the door a neighbour was coming out. "Isn't the news great? The little lad is out of the woods, God be thanked. I'll be off now. I just left a couple of eggs there on the table. He'll need building up, you know." She patted my arm, beaming with relief. "I'll say a few prayers of thanksgiving at mass tomorrow."

Off she went, and I stood for a minute trying to pull myself together. Inside the house my father was with the little lad, trying to get him to drink something. He wasn't interested, he who would normally drink anything. Somehow he looked as though he'd returned from somewhere far off and was still halfway there.

"How's the lad?" I asked, sitting down beside him on the bed. His attempt at a smile wrenched something deep inside me. He was as white as the sheet over him, dark blue bruises under his eyes, his blonde curls matted.

"I got you a bar of chocolate. Your favourite kind. . ." I held it up where he could see. "I'll leave it here on the table for you to eat when you're a bit rested." His eyes lit up for a moment as he saw the chocolate, then his head turned away on the pillow.

"He's tired," my father said. "It was the fever, his temperature was very high, and it has left him weak. He needs a good sleep now."

My father gently settled the pillow a little more comfortably and tucked in the bedclothes. "I'll stay with him for a bit and keep him company. It's been so frightening for him." He drew a scarf over the bedside lamp to stop the glare and settled back in his chair, his eyes on his son in the bed. "You get yourself something to eat."

I found my mother washing clothes in the kitchen, bending over the suddsy water in the big galvanised bath that was balanced on two chairs. The room was full of steam, with a big saucepan of water boiling away on the gas stove. She was singing away to herself to the "thump, thump" of the washing hitting the glass-lined washboard. She straightened up to ease her back as I went in and wiped the sweat off her forehead with one suds-laden hand. I wiped the suds away with the back of my hand.

"Good news," she said. "The pills are working. We could see the fever leaving him, but he's very weak. We'll have to be careful." She bent back over the bath and got back into her rhythm. "I thought I'd get this job out of the way tonight. I couldn't settle to anything all day. There are sheets and things to do. Can you get yourself something to eat? You must be starving. I left the makings there on the table."

I started to fold the things to be left to dry on the clothes horse overnight. Our mangle was too big and awkward to have in the house, so we could only wring out heavy things in the yard in daylight. "That's all right. I had a sandwich."

The "thump, thump" stopped and she stood, easing her back with one sudsy hand, her eyes on mine. "I was kicking myself at not giving you your bus fare this morning, but I was so worried. How had you enough for a sandwich?"

"I had some money of my own," I started, but she wasn't buying that. So I started to give an edited account of my day as she resumed her "thump, thump" against the washboard while the clothes we wrung out together piled up like snakes in the small bath.

"This tick in the shop, and the sandwich. How did that come about?"

I told her and she straightened again.

"Don't do it, child," she said very seriously. "Don't get into that. It's plain and straight. We can't have what we can't pay for. There are things I'd love, but payback time comes all too soon. No point in having half your wages spent before you get it into your hand. I know it's tempting, but if we get into debt there's no way out. Just think of the women going each Monday to the pawn, putting the stuff in and getting it out on Friday. That's no way to live. Nothing's your own, but each of those women started that as a once off. They never thought it'd end up as a Monday morning ritual, but now there's no way out for them. I wouldn't want to see you. . ." She bent again over the steamy bath, thumping away. She looked at me sideways.

"How are you getting on with the older woman?"

I jiggled from one foot to the other, trying to be honest but diplomatic too. This was difficult to answer truthfully.

"All right, I think," I said cautiously.

"M'm. She's probably not the easiest, but you've stepped on to her turf. Don't forget that."

I nodded as we twisted the sheet to get the water out and then coiled it into the small bath. We tidied up the washing and then started to bail out the bath into the sink to ease carrying it away. Together we lifted the now lighter bath out to the yard, emptied it and hung it on its appointed nail, with the smaller bath alongside. Then we opened the window to let the steam out, and I put the kettle on the stove to make a pot of tea. Under a cloth she'd left a cold meat salad, and we had our tea companionably together. On our second cup, she took her purse out of the pocket of her apron, and I couldn't help but notice how thin it was. She took out two shillings and handed them to me.

"No tick and no charity. All right? And I'm sorry it can't be more."

I got out my little purse and showed it to her.

"Tomorrow's Wednesday and I'm halfway to pay day. I've nearly enough to last me out, but I'll get out some of my money from the Post Office before work tomorrow. That will do me grand until Friday, and then I can splurge."

I handed her back the two shillings, and I saw the shamed look of relief on her face as she returned it to her purse. I knew in my heart of hearts that no way in the future would we be thinking in terms of splurges.

Next morning I was a little late getting in to work, having had to wait till our post office opened to get out the money, but nestling in my purse with the other few coins was five whole shillings. That should be enough to make sure I'd pay my own way and not depend on others.

Sadie looked up with some disapproval as I put away my coat and waited to be told what to do. Jim, however, nodded and smiled, and soon I was ensconced at my corner of the table with my column of figures marching with determination down the page, all guns rigidly in line. Jim sat at the other end of the table opening his letters, answering the phone and checking through some files. Then he got up and put on his coat.

"I'm away. No rest for the wicked! Back to Burton's to see can we work out something. Now, there's just two things I've to say before I go."

I sat on the edge of my chair, my eyes fixed on him, wondering what on earth was coming. Could it be?

He smiled. "Nothing to worry about, I assure you. No, it's just that I'm getting a typewriter from head office. Somebody

will drop it in to the Hall during the day. I'd like you to have a
go at it. You see, I don't know what it's like, why it's been dis-
carded, or if it'll work all right. It'd be nice to have a few letters typed and not to have to farm them out. So, what do you
think?"

"I'd be glad to."

"Right. It'll do for the time being on the table here, but we'll
have to get a desk for you, somewhere to put it so that you can
work away in peace. I've had a word with Terry. There's loads of
stuff he's stacked away. Hopefully we'll get something suitable."

He sifted through his letters and handed one to me.

"That letter is for Tommy McCarthy next door. There's
nobody there now, but at about half-ten would you drop it in to
him?"

"Certainly." The sense of relief was immense, and I drew a
deep breath and sat back in the chair. He smiled and went on
his way.

Outside Sadie had some people with her, and I could hear the
murmur of voices and the phone ringing now and again. I concentrated on my army moving in serried ranks down the page.
Now they were several columns wide and as uniform as I could
make them, but I didn't neglect to keep a wary eye on the fire
and feed its hunger for coal. God, it must cost the union a mint
of money to keep the office stocked up with the best kind of coal.

At half-ten I picked up the letter for Tommy McCarthy and
ventured out into the corridor that ran right through the building from the Customs House side to our bit at Eden Quay.

The corridor was long, straight and very dark, with closed
doors leading on to it on both sides. The lighting was minimal,
with just a few weak bulbs dotted here and there. There were no
windows, and the ceiling was much lower than I'd seen before.
Presumably, the rooms alongside this corridor would have been

the bedrooms when this was a hotel. I didn't envy the guests! I knocked on the first door on my left.

"Come in if you're beautiful," a male voice said.

I pushed open the door and walked into the room. The fire was the first thing to draw my eye. It was a big fireplace and it was crammed with red glowing coals, just like something on a Christmas card. The heat was immense. It hit you immediately, taking your breath away; you could almost touch it. The atmosphere was so suffocating that I was tempted to back out to the corridor in self-defence.

Tommy McCarthy was sitting at a desk beside the fire, his chair tilted back on two legs, his feet sprawled on the desk, a phone clamped to his ear. He smiled and nodded at me, indicating I should sit down while he finished his call.

I pulled out a chair, cleared the stuff off it and sat down. Tommy's conversation seemed to require at a minimum one swear word to about every six words spoken.

"So you fuckin' should. . .!"

"I will in my arse. . .!"

"Piss off, you ignorant pig. . .!"

I looked around the room, trying to ignore the swearing. It was a replica of the room I worked in: same windows, same size, but it was dark, no lights or at least no lights on. Against the back wall was an array of silvery objects high up. I squinted to make out their shapes. They were shovels, their silvery heads up, their handles down, maybe twenty of them. Why? I had no idea.

The table in the corner must be Paddy McLoughlin's, the stuff piled neatly, the books stacked. The wall behind his table was totally covered by a kind of linen picture with writing and figures emblazoned on it.

I was trying to read the words when Tommy signalled the end

of his conversation by banging down the phone, removing his feet from the desk and thumping his chair down so that all four legs stood on the floor.

"Sorry about the French—habit, you see. Not being used to being visited by beautiful young ladies at this hour of the morning. I'll have to mend my manners."

He moved to the door. "Golly," he shouted. I swear that his shout could have been heard down at the port. "Golly, you ould reprobate, we have a visitor. Come in quick and show your face!" Somewhere down the corridor an equally loud "Coming" echoed in the confined space.

Tommy smiled and came back to the fire to stand, one foot on the fender. I wondered how on earth he didn't fry!

"You were looking at our banner," he said, pointing to the linen picture. "That's our branch banner, the building workers, you see, doing their bit to make this nation great."

Unexpectedly he started to sing.

> "The Soviet flag is deepest red,
> It shelters all our martyred dead,
> And there their limbs grow stiff and cold,
> Their lifeblood dyes its every fold."

He sang loudly, if not tunefully, and his voice filled every nook and cranny of the room. I sat, mouth open in disbelief. A man came in the door almost silently.

"Tommy, Tommy, can I not leave you for a minute without you making a show of yourself? You've frightened the child. She's scared stiff."

In truth, it wasn't Tommy that had frightened me. It was the man himself. He was huge. He had to bend his head to come in the door, but he also had to come in sideways because of the breadth of his shoulders. He was whispering, I suppose, in his terms, but it was like being in a gale-force wind. He extended his hand to me, and it was like holding a ham haunch.

"The name's Golly," he said, the sound hitting me like a hammer blow. "And yours?"

"I'm May O'Brien," I said and stood up, my eyes reaching somewhere around his midriff. My hand was enveloped inside this gigantic bear's paw that could, if he were so minded, pulverise it, but he held it delicately, like a flower.

I handed the letter to Tommy. "It was in our post," I said, and turned to go.

Tommy tore it open, and after skimming through it, threw the letter on to his desk where it just became part of the accumulation of rubbish.

"Next time we'll give you tea," he pronounced, resuming his place at the desk. "When young ladies call, it's the custom to give them tea. Isn't that right, Golly?"

Golly's smile was way above my head, but I felt his goodwill. "Yes," he said simply. "With cream cakes." He politely held the door open for me to make my departure.

Back in my office I sat dumbfounded. Somehow it was very hard to marshal my army into their places as my brain churned over my visit to the room next door. What could you make of it? There was the heat. How could anyone stick it? There was Tommy's attitude. Could he have a few jars on him? I didn't know, but it was strange. And Golly! He was huge physically, but he'd also this enormous personality. It filled the room to overflowing and made Tommy seem ordinary. Yet he could seem to turn it off or on at will. And the room! The darkness! The shovels with their heads all polished! The banner thing and the song! Who'd ever believe?

My thoughts were cut short abruptly by a kick on the door, a hand fumbling to open it and a muttered swear word. In came

Terry lugging a typewriter with some difficulty.

"Where?"

I cleared a space for him and he banged the typewriter down.

"Poxy stairs," I think he said. There was a string of words I couldn't follow as again he went through the paroxysm of his stammering. When it eased he took a pipe out of his pocket and began to fill it, using a penknife to cut off a piece from a wedge of tobacco, then cutting it small with his knife against the palm of his hand. When it was to his liking, he began to fill the pipe, tamping it down with his thumb, then lighting it with what seemed like a blowtorch. When he had it going satisfactorily, he took a little lid out of his pocket, put it on to the bowl, clamped it tight and turned the pipe so that it faced down. Why, I don't know.

Then he stood comfortably leaning against the wall, puffing away, and the aromatic smell of the tobacco filled the air.

"Going to use that yoke?" he asked between puffs. "It's banjaxed, you know."

"How d'you know? Did you try it?" He fell into a paroxysm of coughing, spluttering and gurgling, bending almost in two to get his breath. He was laughing but not stammering, I noticed.

"Me, try it! That's good, that is! Me, try it! I'm only the bleedin' caretaker, not the bleedin' typist." He thought that was terribly funny.

I banged a few keys at random and it seemed OK, if a bit stiff. "It seems all right, but what about a desk? I have to have somewhere to put it."

He went on smoking, standing stock-still like a statue, the only movement the puffs of smoke drifting towards the ceiling. I waited.

"A desk? What d'ye think I am? Bleedin' Clery's where you only need to say what you want and it's delivered?"

"Jim said you'd see me right. . ."

Reluctantly a little smile appeared in those black buttoney eyes and the puffing reduced in volume.

"What do ye want?"

"A desk or a table to put the typewriter on. I can't work here. It'd drive Jim demented. And a few bits and pieces."

"That's all?" He made gurgling noises with his pipe.

"I could think of more if you want," I offered.

"Bet you could," he chuckled and doused the pipe. "I'll see what I can do."

"Today. I need it today. I can't work here on Jim's table."

He paused in the doorway. "M'm. . .Well, I make no promises, but I'll see what I can do. Maybe something to tide you over, then something better later."

He rooted in his jacket pocket and took something out.

"Ye'll need that, I'm thinking. A little can of oil to loosen things up, and a little steel brush to clean the keys. That should do the trick."

When Sadie came in with a cup of tea, her meeting having finished, she looked at the typewriter with some surprise.

"Terry brought it up?"

"Yes, and he's supposed to bring a desk or a table later today. I suppose it will have to be outside. The pecking here would drive Jim mad otherwise."

She looked at the typewriter appraisingly. "Yes, the outside room at the window. I suppose that's the best place. It's a pity the phone couldn't be extended, and then you could take the calls. Well, don't hold your breath. Terry, well, he's a law to himself."

When I came back at half-two, Terry was sandpapering down a desk, and standing proudly on it was my typewriter, a ream of paper, a box of carbon paper, a stapler, a box of envelopes and a penholder. I was dumbfounded. Terry said nothing for a minute, watching my reaction with a glint of satisfaction. "There's a bit of the veneer got a knock here, so I'll smooth it off. There's no woodworm, so that's OK. I've given it a rub-over so it's quite clean.

"I didn't think. . ." I stammered.

"Didn't think I'd do it, did ye?" he grinned. "By the way, I got the stationery stuff from the cupboard in 'Two-Gun' O'Reilly's office. Borrowed it, you might say. So the less said the better. All right?"

"Robbed it?"

"Some folks are terrible hurtful," he grinned. "Sure all our smoke goes up the same chimney!"

With that he was gone. God, he was really good at this disappearing act.

CHAPTER FIVE

I SAT AT my desk in the window, grinning. I rearranged the things around me, trying to get the best and most efficient lay-out. I was like a child on Christmas morning not wanting to open the present because of the sheer pleasure of feasting one's eyes on it in all its festive glory.

"The idea is to use it, not sit and admire it," Sadie said dryly. "That's what it's for."

So I set to work. I put a sheet of newspaper under the type-writer, got some hot water from the kettle, a rag and a bottle of Ajax from the cleaner's cache, and washed the machine down, drying it carefully. With the little oil can I oiled the moving parts until they moved more freely, then cleaned the keyboard. Then I attacked all my Os and Cs and Ds with the steel brush and an improvised poker made from a straightened paperclip to get out the dirt that clogged up their middles.

I tried typing, checking to make sure that I had no smudged lettering and attacking the offender with the steel brush where necessary.

From time to time the keys all jammed together so that very odd combinations of letters appeared on my bit of paper, but I knew I could deal with that as I became more accustomed to the feel of the keyboard.

"I'm off up town," Sadie said and departed abruptly.

In truth, I didn't blame her. It must have driven her berserk to have me pecking at the keyboard, with pauses, exclamations, and then a crescendo of noise as I attempted to get some speed up. The typewriter had a kind of sit-up-and-beg look about it, but it worked all right. There were a few interruptions—phone calls, visitors and, of course, my role as stoker to the two fires—but the pleasure of sitting there before my new typewriter and seeing the printed page appear with gradually fewer errors outweighed everything else. Paddy McLoughlin came in and slouched over the counter, watching me with amusement.

"I came to see the woodpecker," he said with a grin. "Tap-tap, tap-tap, tappity-tap-tap; we thought we'd been invaded by birds. Bad enough to be eaten by woodworm, but to be tapped to death by wood-peckers, that'd be the pits."

"Terry brought it," I grinned, "and the desk too. Isn't it great?"

"And the paper and that too? Now, I wonder where he robbed that from?"

My hands on the keys stopped abruptly.

"You mean. . ."

"Well, the typewriter is a throw-out from head office. The desk is part of the stuff he stashed away when he cleared out some of the rooms that are off-limits, but where could he have got the stationery? Everything here is padlocked, stands to reason. Your coal shed, for instance. If it wasn't, a half a dozen jokers would be sitting at home with their feet on the mantelpiece toasting themselves."

"But. . ." With a sinking heart I remembered Terry's reference. "He said something about 'Two-Gun' O'Reilly, and that the less said about the stationery the better."

"Tom?" Paddy threw back his head and laughed. "God, if

'Two-Gun' finds Terry raided his stationery press, he'll have his guts for garters. He really will pin his hide to the wall."

"But. . ." I didn't know what to say. Memories of films about gangland warfare and people being mown down by bursts of machine-gun fire were deeply engrained in my mind. Could this "Two-Gun" name actually mean a man could be armed and would shoot Terry? The phone ringing in his office caused Paddy's reluctant departure, and I went back to my keyboard somewhat chastened.

At around five o'clock Jim returned and I gave him his messages. He smiled to see me ensconced with my new equipment.

"Well, well," he grinned. "We are really getting in line with the times at last. You can manage it OK? It is in working order?"

I showed him some samples of my work, and he pretended to examine them critically.

"I'll leave you a few letters to do tomorrow," he said. "And there's the branch committee minutes too. Sure, I won't know myself not having to go, hat in hand, and get somebody to type stuff for the branch."

"Terry. . . Well, he brought the typewriter and the desk, and the stationery too. Will he be in trouble about the stationery? He said something about a man called 'Two-Gun' O'Reilly?"

"Tom O'Reilly?" He chuckled, finding the idea amusing, but I didn't. "Child, Terry is an enigma even to those who know him well. I wouldn't worry your head about the stationery. If Terry really wanted to, he'd get into Fort Knox. Padlocks to Terry are child's play. Tom O'Reilly boasted that his office was securely locked. Terry has shown him, and us, that it wasn't. It's only a battle of wits, not a bloodbath. You can rest easy on that."

He poked the fire and put more coal on.

"I'll be late here tonight. Some work that has to be done, but what we must do is put things on a proper footing. If you need more stationery, in reason, of course, I'll order it from head office. That's not a problem. That reminds me." He took his wallet from his pocket and peeled of a note, putting it down on the desk.

"We need some petty cash that you can draw on, for stamps or milk or whatever. You draw on it as you need, and if you need more, just ask me." He took a little tin cashbox out of a drawer and handed me the key. Then he got out a brand-new jotter and wrote across the cover:

PETTY CASH BOOK

"You write in what you spend and balance it at the end of the week. You give it to me on Monday morning. I keep Monday morning free usually to do the branch accounts, making sure everything balances. We're responsible to the members, you see."

I put the money in the box, locked it, and put it away in one of my drawers, swallowing the lump in my throat.

"I will. I'll look after it, Jim."

"Right. Another of life's obstacles surmounted. And we've a possible solution to the Burton problem. The company have offered a token payment to the pressers and machinists, not enough in their view, but still there is an opportunity for overtime. That'll give them higher earnings than day work, and the cutters will pull out all the stops to get enough work through to keep them going full-belt. So, barring the usual mouth throwing a spanner in the works, that should solve the problem."

"But it never stops. . ." The words were out before I could stop them. Jim looked at me in surprise.

"But that's the job. In a perfect world we wouldn't be needed. It's when things go wrong we earn our few shillings. For instance, that lad, Joe Lynch, the presser from Fisher's, he's a case in point. He's one of the best pressers in the trade, but he drinks too much. Not all the time, but out of the blue he goes on the batter, doesn't get into work and gets sacked. You can understand old man Fisher. He's got a small place; the work is geared to go through fast to save costs. He's paid when he delivers the suit or whatever to the shop.

"Joe's hand is the last hand to touch the work. At his best he makes it look top class. When he's not there, the work can't go out, and Fisher isn't paid, but he has to pay the wages. It's a spiral, but the real victim is Joe, and as time goes by he'll become unemployable. Nobody'll want him."

He glanced at the clock. "It's getting late. Off you go and we'll do a few letters tomorrow. All right?"

I nodded, put the cover on my typewriter, and said my "Goodnight", leaving him bent over his desk totally immersed in some new problem.

In the bus on my way home, I could hardly stop grinning like an idiot. I would now be abandoning my soldiers marching down the page in favour of typing real-life letters on that union letter-headed paper and posting the letters in the pillar-box outside the hall door. I was in charge of the petty cash; a whole pound was in the box. I would have to balance the account every week and make sure I never forgot to note my debits as against my credits. I sighed in contentment.

At home things too were much brighter. The lad was sitting up in bed; comics loaned by neighbours' kids were being read voraciously, with an odd explanatory aside from my father.

"So, how was your day?" my mother asked as we washed up after the tea.

"Great! I've a typewriter now and a desk to myself, stationery, and I'm going to type real letters tomorrow. I'm in charge of the petty cash to buy stamps and milk and all that. It's great!"

She smiled at my enthusiasm.

"The lad is much better," she said contentedly. "He's had a second helping of rice pudding, and he was up for a half-hour. It'll take time and we'll have to make sure he doesn't try to rush things." She hung her apron on the back of the door and smoothed her hair with her hand.

"God is good, all the same!" she said, half-seriously.

"And the devil's not such a bad fellow," I responded with the usual family rejoinder. We both smiled, and knew exactly what we meant.

CHAPTER SIX

N EXT MORNING I could hardly wait to get into work to make
sure my new equipment was still there. In fact, I was in the
hall when the cleaner was sweeping down the wooden stairs.

"Early bird, aren't you?" she said. "It doesn't last long, believe
me." She stood leaning on her brush, smiling pityingly as I
rushed up the stairs two at a time.

When I reached the office the typewriter stood there on the
desk with my stuff all around it just as I'd left it the evening
before. On the desk in front of my chair was a little mound of
paper. I checked it quickly: three letters written by Jim Gilhooley addressed to head office, Burton's and the employers' organisation. I read through them quickly, before I'd even hung up
my coat. I could read the handwriting, so that was OK. I'd to do
copies and enclose them as directed. That was OK too.

One thing threw me though. The head office letter was
addressed to the general secretary, but it started "Dear Comrade" and it ended "Yours fraternally". Did they really do that?
It certainly was something we had never done in our typing class
in the Tech, but maybe unions were different. I ran down to the
shop. The little wispy woman came to me and smiled enquiringly. Close up, she was the image of the little spinster teacher
in the cowboy films: small, slight, grey hair in a bun with stray

bits falling to her face, wire-rimmed glasses, faded mild-blue eyes and a rather prim expression.

"Ah, you're with Jim Gilhooley?" Her voice fitted her looks completely, mild, hesitant, almost a whisper.

"Yes," I nodded. "I've to hurry. I want a half pint of milk and a packet of Jacob's Goldgrain biscuits, please. It's for the office, so can I pay on Friday?"

"So you want tick?" she asked mildly, taking a book down from a shelf and licking the lead of a pencil.

"No, it's on account," I said. "I've my Petty Cash book here, and I'll make the entry and keep my debits and credits in order each day. It's how we were taught in the Tech. It's a business account."

As she rang up the transaction on the till, I put the amounts into my book as a debit against the one pound credit. I looked up as I noticed the silence and found everyone looking at me. "This way we all know how we stand," I said briskly, taking up my purchases. "I'll come in each morning before work for the milk. Is that all right, Mrs. . .?"

"Rosie," she said, trying to keep a smile from her lips. "Rosie's my name, and I'm glad to have your account. That's very good business practice." She reached her hand out and took mine. "It's a deal."

Back in the office, coat disposed of, fires checked, purchases put away, I sat down, took the Irish Transport and General Workers' Union headed paper, put in my carbon and backing sheet, and started typing.

I can't say that any of the three letters when finished were perfect typing examples. My teacher would have had something to say about the spacing and the layout, not to mention the "Dear Comrade", but that aside they were good and I'd done exactly what Jim had said. I looked at them proudly, and then laid them on Jim's desk, envelopes linking each letter with enclosed copy and a filing copy.

I was tidying up things when the door opened and a woman walked in. She was young, petite, thin, with high heels and make-up. She was dressed in a short skirt, ivory satin blouse, and her hair was permed. Over her shoulder she carried a leather satchel handbag.

"Can I help you?" I asked.

Uninvited, she came in behind the counter and stood beside me looking at my new equipment.

"Time the branch got itself up to date," she said. "I'm bloody fed up doing letters for them. Is it any good?" She rattled a drum rat-tat-tat on the keys so fast you could hardly see her fingers move. "Not so bad," she confirmed. "Hasn't been used recently, so it's a little tight, but a bit of use and it'll go a tidy trot."

She looked around appraisingly. "You need a press—a lock-up to keep the stuff in."

She peered into various presses, and I wondered whether to object. "That'll do. Just clear the stuff and it'll be handy enough. Get Terry to do the lock. That will be a bit of the poacher turned gamekeeper, but, sure, if he wants to get into a press, he will."

She noticed my concerned face. "Oh God, I didn't introduce myself. I'm Frances Lambert. I work down in the Hotel Branch on the ground floor beside the shop. It's an awful kip, but then they all are. It's time they finished the job those British shells started in 1916."

I told her my name and we shook hands.

"How old are you?" she asked.

"Why?"

"Just to make you realise I'm senior to you," she laughed. "No, seriously, we're the only young people in this whole set-up.

They're all over the hill here. Not that I'd want to work in that
head office place; they're all Holy Marys over there. They were
old years before their time." She opened the handbag, and
make-up, a hairbrush, nail varnish and lipstick fell out.

"You'll have to come down and see my place for yourself. I
couldn't describe it. You see, the casuals have to sign in and wait
to be jobbed for the functions, like weddings and that."

She rooted around in the bag and took out a paper bag. "I've
got you a few bits and pieces that might be handy. See, like these
stencils for doing copies, and a bit of copying paper and a half-
used bottle of correcting fluid. That looks like nail varnish, but
it's not, so don't put it on your nails!" She laughed at her own
joke. "If you need anything else, come down to me."

I thanked her, and she stuffed her things back into her handbag.

"That's all right," she said, making for the door, then paused.
"Oh, you'll need to get a rubber stamp made of Jumbo's name,
his signature, for circulars and that. Head office will do that. I've
also brought you a few stamps to start you off." Out of her bag
she produced six stamps and handed them to me. "You'll need
to get your stuff into the post box by five o'clock to catch the
evening post."

With that she was gone, and I could hear the high heels make
a staccato drumbeat across the wooden floor outside. I looked
at the press she had indicated and knew she was right, but wondered if I should move stuff that was already there. A sound
made me look up, and there was Sadie looking down at me
grimly.

"And what do you think you're doing with that press?" she
asked, her voice icy with disapproval.

"The stationery, I have to have somewhere to put it. Frances
said. . ."

"You didn't think to ask what Sadie said. I say what goes where in this office. Don't you forget that! What was that young one doing up here anyway? It would be better if she'd mind her own business."

"She just came to say hello." I said.

"So she said it. That's the end of the matter. I believe you've more posting to do. Just do it." She turned on her heel and went out, annoyance showing in every movement she made.

I was completely taken aback. Obviously I had to do what she said, but it seemed awfully unfair. She seemed to actively dislike Frances for some reason. I mightn't exactly like her, but she had been kind, and I appreciated that. Disconsolately I stacked the stationery up on chairs, lifted the typewriter to a chair in the corner, and got my army on the move once more.

Jim came in after lunch and I waited, wondering what he'd think of my first letters. He came to the door and called me into his office, closing the door after me and telling me to sit down in the chair opposite him. I waited, my heart in my mouth.

"Nothing to worry about," he said affably. "The letters are grand, but I wanted to have a word with you." He signed the letters and passed them back to me, and I couldn't help noticing what a nice elegant signature he had.

"You've an account in the shop, I understand?" he commented off-handedly.

"Yes, it seemed the best way to keep things clear cut, and I'll get more stamps tomorrow morning. A woman called Frances Lambert gave me some to start me off, but I have to pay her back or her books will be wrong."

"Exactly. Now, there are a couple of things we've got to get clear. I'll pay you your wages tomorrow morning at ten o'clock. We'll do that each week as far as we can. If I'm away, I'll leave it in your desk drawer in an envelope. I've told head office that

I'm perfectly happy with your work so they'll do the paperwork, tax, social welfare and so on. Of course, you'll have to join the union as a staff member. So there'll be deductions from your wages but not just yet. Do you understand that?"

I nodded. My visions of going home with my thirty shillings in my little purse taking a bit of a nose-dive.

"I've talked to the finance people, and when the deductions are made your wages will go up to compensate. I think that's only fair. You have to do a month's probation, but unless you do something spectacularly wrong, that's more of a bureaucratic detail than anything else. So that's that."

He took a big leather-bound folder from a press and sat down again. "Do you know anything about minutes of meetings?" he asked.

I thought for a moment. "You mean, reports. . .?"

"Yes, but more specific than that. I've a branch committee meeting on Monday night. I take notes at that meeting about decisions, arguments, all that, and I've to transcribe them later into minutes, as an account of what has happened. Then that's typed out and put into this minute book. I read it to the meeting, its adoption is proposed, and if it's accepted and the chairman signs it, it then becomes a legally binding document. You see how important it is that it be totally accurate?"

I nodded. I could see what he meant, but I knew nothing about how the union operated.

He looked at me appraisingly. "You want to know how it works?"

"Yes. There's so much I don't know. . ."

"We'll take it in easy stages," he joked. "Let's see now. I don't want to put you off the whole thing."

He took a box of paper clips and held it up. "These clips are workers. This is make-belief, you understand?" He spilled the clips out on to the table and divided them in half, pushing one group aside.

"These are non-union. They have no voice. They must accept whatever the boss man decides even if it means a cut in wages."

He divided the other group into small piles. "These are union people, in different branches throughout the country: miners, busmen, labourers, factory workers, hospital workers, etc. All with one voice."

He took one of the little piles and drew it forward.

"This is our branch, clothing workers, well, wider than that really. Textiles, knitwear, hosiery, laundries, dry cleaning: a broad group, about 3,000. Each factory has a shop steward, a spokesperson they elect to speak for them. They deal with minor issues on the factory floor, and they collect the union money. That's the money you've been putting into the register. They come in on Friday afternoon, Saturday morning and Monday night with their money. Incidentally, for now you won't be asked to work on Saturday mornings. We'll break you in gradually on handling the money. There is an lot of procedure involved, and it's too early to give you that responsibility."

He moved the clips around.

"Because we meet most shop stewards weekly, we know what's happening in most of those factories. We also have a branch committee. The members elect delegates to represent them collectively. Almost all factories in the branch are involved." He drew out a small cluster of paper clips and formed them into a line, then drew out one clip.

"That's me as branch secretary. I put into effect what the branch committee recommends as far as I can, and I'm answerable to them. I deal with problems on the work floor and try to do what head office wants."

He drew out small groups from the other groups of clips.

"These are all the other branches around the country. They've all got their branch committees too in their own areas of employment, but to make sure all views can be put together from all over the country there's another strand, and that's the national executive council who are elected nationally."

He moved that group forward to form a smaller circle.

"Then there are the Annual National Conferences where the delegates from the branches debate policy, but we'll leave that aside for the moment."

He drew three clips and put them together, one in front.

"These are the three officers: the general president, Billy McMullen (you spoke to him on the phone), the vice president and the general secretary. They are the top three with total responsibility. They have to make sure the ship is sailing in the right direction and that all the crew are pulling together. We're that crew, paid by the members to bring that ship safely to port."

He tipped the clips into his hand and then put them into the box.

"You understand the basic necessity is accountability. We all have to be accountable for what we do, mistakes or otherwise."

He stood up, back to the fire, warming himself.

"What's this thing about the press outside?"

I gaped at him for a moment, totally dumbfounded. "You mean. . ."

"The press, child, the press. . ."

"Oh! Frances Lambert came in. I'd never met her before, but she brought me a few things, stencils and stamps. Things she thought might help me get started. She said to get a press to put the stuff into to keep it safe and to get Terry to put a lock on it. I was looking at the press, just looking. I hadn't touched anything, but Sadie was very annoyed. I don't really know why."

"M'm." He rubbed his hands before the fire, warming them.

"Change is difficult, it's hard to accept. We all react in our own way, not always with our heads, more with our hearts. The union is changing. It has to or be left behind with the dinosaurs. The changes in the office are only a symptom. Typewriters, where before handwritten stuff was good enough, reports in triplicate, accounts being scrutinised, rules that seem petty when for many of us workplace issues are far more pressing. This sort of pressure comes when an organisation of idealistic voluntary amateurs with dreams is forced into becoming a professional body. This stuff has nothing to do with you, child. You just do the job you're trained to do. Our problem is that we're trained for nothing but expected to do everything."

He smiled and sat down again.

"Now where was I? Oh yes, the minutes."

He handed me a hard-backed notebook filled with writing.

"It might just help if a word puzzles you. Now, here's the script you use."

He handed me a handwritten, six-page document.

"You type it like this."

He handed me the leather-covered folder.

"This is the special paper."

He handed me a half box of paper.

"All this is confidential, you understand that?"

He smiled and picked up the phone, and I stood up, knowing our meeting was over.

"Have it ready on Monday at two o'clock. That's a priority. I'll mention it to Sadie. All right?"

I smiled and took the stuff in my arms and went back to my desk outside, my brain on fire with so much stuff given in so short a time. I put away the register and put back up my typewriter and stuff on the desk, then checked through Jim's handwriting.

It was difficult at first to make head or tail of it because of the use of jargon I had never heard before. I started to type, gaining confidence as I got into the sense of it. Sadie came over and put a cup of tea down on the desk. "I'll get Mrs Hanratty to clear out that press," she said. "You can't have that stuff strewn all over the place. I'll get Terry to put a lock on the door to keep it secure. Fat chance of that, I suppose. Anything that's not nailed down walks away in here!"

I breathed a sigh of relief. This was better. Jim had obviously had a word with her, and things were easier between us. Why was she so antagonistic to Frances? That seemed to make no sense.

I was determined to have the minutes typed, perfect and in exactly the same format as Jim wanted, by the next day. However, towards the end of the evening there was an interruption.

Frank Robbins came hurrying in. "Jumbo," he called to Jim in the next room. "Where the hell are you? Would you ever come out here?"

Jim came out, rubbing his glasses with his handkerchief. "What's the fuss? What d'ye want, Frank?"

"It's bad news, Jumbo. Tom Kennedy is dead. The funeral is tomorrow to Glasnevin after ten o'clock mass. We have work to do, Jumbo. I'll give a shout to Tommy McCarthy."

He did that literally.

"Tommy, Tommy, get your arse in here, pronto," he yelled down the corridor. "Tell the rest to come in here. There's work to be done."

He turned to Sadie. "Will you tell Rosie and Peg O'Donnell? You know what to do." She left immediately, putting her coat on as she went. Down the corridor there was the sound of doors banging and voices raised as the call went out: "Something is wrong." Then people began to congregate around the open door asking what the hell was wrong, why all the shouting. Jim took over.

"Inside into my office, the lot of you. Frank will explain the arrangements. The news is that Tom Kennedy is dead." The men all crowded inside Jim's office and Frank began to speak. Jim came out to me.

"It's a bit of an emergency. Will you take over? Take messages; do whatever is needed? There may be some membership money paid in this evening. If there is, just check how much the shop steward's book totals, that the cash is the same, and then sign the receipt in the back of the book. Lock the whole lot away in your desk drawer for tonight. Here's the key for the office; lock up when you're going. All right?"

I nodded. In the inside office voices were raised, questions asked, latecomers briefed; then people began to drift away to do whatever they'd been called upon to do. Soon silence reigned, and I sat on, making sure that the fires were fuelled and the phones answered. When a shop steward arrived to pay contributions, I managed, with her help, to make sense of the procedure and do what was necessary without too much trouble.

In the bus going home, I had plenty to occupy my mind, so that I was surprised when a neighbour spoke to me.

"You were away in a world of your own," she laughed. "I suppose that's not to be wondered at when you're so happy about the little lad."

For a moment I was so taken aback I could only gape at her. In truth, I had to admit to myself that I'd never, all day, thought about him, or about home, or how they were faring. So much had happened, and the day had seemed so short.

"Ah, well, then maybe it's love," the woman laughed as we got off the bus. "Sure, you're only young once. Make the most of it, child."

As I trudged home there were a number of things on my mind. My job was OK and I'd have most of my thirty shillings in my little purse tomorrow morning. I knew all too well what that meant to my family. To get the little things that would make recovery easier for the lad meant we would all need to contribute something more. For my mother it meant cutting costs wherever she could because my father's wages were set and wouldn't move up, whatever about moving down. My mother had even talked about a cleaning job for herself to bring in the extra few pounds needed.

Did it have to be like this? For the first time in my life, I wondered why it seemed to be set in stone that some people should have to struggle to just exist while others lived in the lap of luxury. I remembered when we had lived in a gate lodge on an estate where my father drove the owner and his family around in posh cars. I had learned to accept that for the children of that family life was easy and very different from mine.

I would never have the clothes, the toys, the education, the things that made up their lives, but I had never envied them. However, I did resent their casual assumption that we were somehow part of their possessions. We were there to open the gate, to be patronised and to be played with only when nobody of their own class was available and to have their things passed down to us when they tired of them.

Now suddenly there seemed to be an alternative idea, quite revolutionary to me. People like Jim Gilhooley could be a spokesman for the workers. He saw them as having rights, not having to accept their role as second-class citizens. I have to admit in truth it was something akin to love that suddenly popped up in my life. This was not the romantic stuff one saw on the wide screen with someone like Myrna Loy, all gooey-eyed, roses round the door, and invisible orchestras playing away in the background, as love found its way through all the obstacles devised by some star-struck script writer.

No. I'd seen, briefly it is true, a very different world where power didn't reside with the wealthy, with the powerful, with the rich, but where all were equal and had the same rights, and this seemed so good to me.

CHAPTER SEVEN

WHEN I TOLD my mother that I had to be in work early because somebody was dead, she looked at me in surprise.

"Who's dead?" she asked, reasonably enough.

"Someone called Tom Kennedy. He must be someone important. They were all running around like headless chickens arranging things. I had to look after everything in the office. I even had to lock up."

My mother looked suitably impressed.

"Jim said I'll get my wages this morning at ten o'clock. So when I get home I'll be a real wage earner."

"We'll have to have a little talk then," she said, patting my arm. "We can't let these riches go to our heads, now can we?" She got on with putting stuff on a plate as attractively as she could for the little lad's breakfast. "But, God, I only wish I could do with less. It's awful needing most of your first wage packet just to keep going."

"Things will get better," I said.

She sighed. "I get the feeling there'll always be something," she muttered to herself. "But God's good."

"And the devil's not such a bad fellow," I responded, and we both smiled at the old joke.

As I crossed Butt Bridge next morning, I thought Liberty Hall looked even worse than usual. It was a grey day with ominous clouds over the Custom House, and our building was dark, squat and almost sinister in its blankness. Then I saw the two flags at half-mast, the Tricolour and the starry blue flag. That must be for the dead man, I thought, and wondered again why he was so important.

In the shop Nellie was alone and it was strangely deserted. The men who usually stood in it were outside at the corner chatting and smoking.

"You're just in time," Nellie said, handing me my milk. "The shop will be shut in a few minutes. Rosie is going to the funeral. God, she's very upset."

Upstairs in the office, Mrs Hanratty was grimly cleaning up a very real mess. There were used cups, glasses, half-eaten sandwiches, ashtrays filled to overflowing and cigarette butts heeled out on the floor. The fire a grey mass of cinders.

"What's happened?" I asked, putting down my things and looking around in dismay.

"A wake, I'm thinking. The bastards! D'ye think they'd treat their own homes like this?" she said as she attacked the fire fiercely with the poker. "Maybe they would. They'd have their own skivvy to do the cleaning at home too."

Under her direction we got the place reasonably tidy in about twenty minutes and stood back to check our work.

"Not bad," she said grudgingly. "It'll do in the circumstances." She bundled her stuff together and went off still muttering about how badly she was being treated. I knew that would be her theme song for the next few weeks. The phone rang and I answered it.

"O'Reilly here," a man's voice said. "Quick message to all staff and any members knocking around. Assemble on the steps of the Hall at 10.45 precisely. Lock your door after you. Wear your coat. It'll be chilly. Is that clear?"

The phone banged down and I stood dumbfounded. Did this instruction apply to me? I looked at the clock, 10.35 already. Was I staff?

Paddy McLoughlin put his head around the door. "Get the call from on high?" I nodded.

"Do as he says," he advised. "It's the funeral, you see. It'll come across Butt Bridge."

I built up the fires, made sure they were safe, took the phone off the hook, put on my coat, and then I thought if someone should come to the hall door on the quay and find it locked they'd be upset. So I took a little meeting card and printed across it "CLOSED FOR FUNERAL" and pinned it to the door, locking it behind me. Then I walked down the long straight corridor to the front of the building.

It was a strange feeling, claustrophobic, I suppose is the best description. The light was poor and the floor was made of boards, some warped, some sagging, so that my progress was accompanied by many creaks and groans. When I reached the end, the place was a sea of activity. There were men lifting things, pushing things, coiling lines and smoothing things on the floor. In the middle of it was Terry, empty pipe upside down in his mouth, a man deferred to by the men around him. A few women stood on one side, dressed in dark clothes, chatting, but they paid me no attention.

I stood at the top of the steps at the front door. Outside was a crowd of people. Men stood chatting and smoking, leaning over the bridge, huddled against the wall of the Liffey, across the road at the Custom House railings and steps.

Suddenly there was a move, at no signal that I saw, and the road in front of Liberty Hall was filled with men. At the same time people crowded on to the steps from the building behind so that there was a crush of bodies trying to get a space. Behind me a man put his arm out to the railings to steady himself.

"You'll be all right, child," he said with a grin. "Just use your elbows. I'm here behind you. I'll see you're OK."

"It's coming!" somebody shouted. "The funeral, it's coming!"

The long black snake of cars was indeed coming down by the river towards us. As the hearse was about to reach the intersection on to Butt Bridge, men stepped out into the traffic, hands upheld to stop the opposite traffic flow. The same thing happened at Eden Quay. One of the men holding up his hand was Golly.

A young lad on a bike tried to sneak past, and Golly, moving very fast for a man of his size, just scooped him up, bike and all, and deposited him on the footpath. The young lad sat dumbstruck. Golly gestured towards the Liffey. The young lad disappeared double-quick into the crowd, and a little cheer went up from the bystanders.

Bus drivers and conductors of stationary buses held up by Golly and company stood chatting, and the bemused passengers crowded around the bus windows to see what was happening.

The hearse stopped just beyond Liberty Hall, the first mourning car leaving a little distance between the two vehicles. Behind it the black cars formed a shiny snake across the bridge and up the quay as far as one could see. Six men stepped forward from the crowd, all wearing black armbands. They lifted the coffin draped with a cloth from the hearse, shouldered it and turned to face Liberty Hall. One of them was Frank Robbins.

A group of perhaps twenty men, with black armbands too, formed a guard of honour, facing the coffin so that it passed between them as it was carried towards the Hall. Jim was there, Tommy McCarthy and some of the men from the shop. The coffin stopped, the guard formed up around it, all facing towards the Hall.

A man came forward with the blue starry flag held at chest level. It was draped with black ribbon at the top, its folds held in the man's hand. At the foot of the coffin, the flag was lowered so that its tip almost touched the ground, and then raised again. The man stepped aside and two men with black armbands moved towards the flag as honour guard.

You could hear a collective sigh rise through the crowd on the steps, and, here and there, men brushed tears away from their cheeks, pretending it was the wind that caused their eyes to water.

From the window up above us, the notes of a flute cut through the air like crystal. At first there seemed to be no recognisable tune; the notes hovered and whirled seemingly at random. Then the melody could be picked out, only to disappear again beneath the grace notes. The player settled into "Roisin Dubh", putting everything he could into his playing. Again there was a collective sigh as the final notes subsided and died in the breeze.

There was total silence for a moment. It felt strange in an assembly of so many people. Down below us a man soothed a little boy held on his shoulder.

A man's voice broke the silence, singing:

> "Oh hear ye the watchword of Labour
> The slogan of they who'd be free
> That no more to any enslaver
> Shall Labour bend suppliant knee.
> That we on whose shoulders are borne
> The pomp and the pride of the great
> Whose toil they repay with their scorn
> Shall challenge and master our fate!"

When the final deep, velvety note died away, again there was a momentary silence, this time broken by a collective clearing of throats. Then all around me everyone joined in the chorus. It was also taken up by those on the opposite side of the road, by the men along the quay walls, and then joined by the men from the cars who'd got out to lend their voices to the Labour anthem.

The welling of sound caused the seagulls along the river to take to the air, squalling their disapproval. Faces peered out of buildings along the quay, wondering what on earth was going on. The mostly male voices massed together and sang their hearts out in their anthem for their dead comrade.

> "Then send it aloft on the breeze, boys!
> That watchword the grandest we've known
> That Labour must rise from its knees, boys,
> And claim the broad earth as its own!"

Again for a few moments there was a silence. Then over our heads a loudspeaker crackled into life and a voice spoke.

"Comrades, this is not the time nor the place to make long speeches. A family is in sorrow, their loss is great, beyond anything mere words can describe. We mustn't make their suffering greater. Tom would never forgive us for that. On behalf of our union, the Irish Transport and General Workers' Union, all I will say is Tom Kennedy was my comrade, in good times and in bad. He was true and staunch, a man amongst men, and he'll be sorely missed by everyone who knew and loved him."

Again there was silence as the voice, choked with emotion, died away.

"Please honour the national anthem," another voice requested.

There was a ripple of sound as hats and caps were doffed, the men in the guard of honour all holding them over their hearts. All turned, as best they could, to the Tricolour flying at half-mast and, led by the bass singer, the national anthem rang out. As the last notes died away, the coffin carried by the six men made its way to the head of the procession, led by the blue starry flag and flanked by the guard of honour. Then, as if on an order, men fell into rank behind it, marching along, arms swinging. The hearse and the cars followed, with some difficulty in trying to keep to the walking pace.

A group of uniformed men swung into step behind the flag, their band instruments covered to show mourning. They moved off at an order from the band master. The solemn heartbeat of the big drum echoed back from the grey surrounding buildings. A rustling sound kept pace with the hearse as men standing in silence doffed their caps. The only movement was the quick sign of the cross as an invocation for the eternal peace of the soul of their dead friend.

As the last car crossed the bridge, the men on point duty waved on the traffic, sauntered back to the pavement and made for the pub, their duty done. Slowly, people drifted away, chatting, meeting friends, sharing memories. Inside the building the dismantling work was going on. Terry was very much in evidence. A big burly man stepped out of a doorway and barred my way, his hand out.

"I'm sorry," he said. "I was a bit abrupt there. I didn't mean it. I'm Tom O'Reilly, No. 3 Branch. Food and all that sort of stuff. That's our share of the membership, for our sins. You're in Clothing with Jim Gilhooley, that's right, isn't it?"

"You were on the phone. . ." My hand was being pumped by the man, but my mind was racing. This was "Two-Gun" O'Reilly, the man whose stationery press Terry had raided. He didn't look a bit like what I expected. I'd thought. . .

"How're you fitting in?"

"All right, I think!"

"Confusing, isn't it? You'll be all right with Jumbo. He's a sound man, none better. Call in to the office some time. It's up there." He waved to somewhere up the stairs and was gone.

I went about my business, trying to get into perspective what had happened. The funeral had been moving. There was no doubt about that. I knew nothing about Tom Kennedy, yet felt he was part of me. That was strange. I'd first heard his name only last night. The way things had been arranged, was it to some formula? I didn't know.

I thought about "Two-Gun" O'Reilly. I'd had a picture in my mind of a cowboy, a kind of film baddie with the black Stetson who shot the hero in the white Stetson from ambush somewhere.

"Two-Gun" had been dressed in sober black with matching waistcoat, white shirt and black tie, a heavy gold watch chain stretched across his ample belly. He was soft spoken in this building where everyone seemed to feel compelled to shout. But there was something shivery about his eyes, pale blue, watchful eyes that would never be surprised by anything and were totally at odds with his bluff hail-fellow-well-met manner.

The others came in, very subdued, after lunch. Jim apologised immediately for not having had my wages ready. He took a pound note and a ten shilling note from his wallet and handed them to me.

"May it be the beginning of many more pay packets from the union," he said with a smile. "It was a difficult start for you and you did very well. From time to time these emergencies arise. It's good to know you can cope."

In the bus going home, I was very conscious of the wages now nestling in my pocket. I wondered how it would be divided.

Maybe a pound for my mother and ten shillings for me? Would that be fair when things were so tight at home?

In bed that night I went over and over again those moments of silence on the steps of Liberty Hall when the man sang the "Watchword" and the feeling the funeral evoked. I thought of the men with tears in the corners of their eyes, the rustle of sound as the hats and caps were removed for the national anthem. It had truly been a day to remember!

On Saturday morning my mother and myself completed our "little talk". She took the thirty shillings I offered her and returned ten shillings to me. "Sorry I have to take that much," she apologised, "but with the little lad's illness, things are a bit tight just now. Maybe in a few weeks. . ."

"That's all right," I said. "Maybe someday I'll get a bike. . ."

"If wishes were horses," she murmured. "We'd all ride to hell," I responded, and we smiled at the absurdity of the old tag.

I gave Con and Kate enough money for the Saturday matinee in the local cinema, and they grabbed it with whoops of joy. My father went even further by producing a bag of sweets, and off they went as happy as Larry to boast of their good fortune to their friends.

I wrestled with my conscience about putting money back in the post office, but my ten shillings was going rapidly and I still had to get something for the little lad. It was heart breaking to see him. He wanted to go out to play with the kids of his age, but he hadn't the strength to keep up with them. He watched them do the things he wanted to do too, and his face had such a yearning look.

I saw my father's eyes on him and knew he had noticed, as I had, that my brother's clothes were now about two sizes too big, his boots too heavy, his hair too dull and long for his thin white little face. I put my arm around him.

"Suppose you had sixpence to spend? What would you buy first?"

He leaned back against me, considering. "Maybe. . ."

I gave him a hug. "What about a Lucky Dip? Or Honeybee toffees? Or a liquorice pipe? Or an ice-cream cone with raspberry on the top? Or a few Jelly Babies?"

After a deal of thinking, he decided on the ice cream and the toffees, and I went off and got them for him, adding a copy of the *Dandy* as my own offering.

He lay down on the bed quite happy with his lot, the ice cream gone in a minute, but the toffees and the comic offering hours of enjoyment still to come.

"Right," my father said, putting down his paper. "We'd better get on with the work while we've a bit of peace." Off he went to get things ready for our next chore, which involved all us near adults in the family.

My father was a thwarted farmer who grew things for the love of seeing them grow, apart altogether from keeping a family fed. He grew tomatoes in butter boxes in the backyard, and every year they would be picked, rolled up in newspaper and placed in strategic places to ripen. They later became an essential part of our menu as tomato soup, usually on a Wednesday. The younger kids thought Wednesday was a special day because the smell was so enticing when they ran home from school, and it was so tasty they would empty the pot in no time. The truth was that Wednesday was the worst day for my mother as she tried to make the coins in her purse stretch to another dinner after the rent was paid on Tuesday. The soup, for her, was the lowest point of her housekeeping week, for the children the highest.

Our task today was the potatoes. My father had a Dublin Corporation plot and he grew vegetables, mainly potatoes, with an odd few chrysanthemums for my mother. When the time was right, he transported the potatoes home, a sack each night balanced on the crossbar of his bike as he walked alongside it. They were carefully stored in the shed in the backyard in layers of peat with old sacks and bits of carpet on top to keep out the frost.

They needed periodic clearing out to remove the bad ones as the months went by. Later he would pick out what he needed for seed potatoes, and they'd be put aside to be planted on St Patrick's Day.

Old sacks were placed on the yard floor. My father and my eldest brother began to scoop the potatoes into buckets and basins from the shed. They were then spilled out on to the sacks and our task began. It was cold. There always seemed to be a cutting east wind when we set about this job, and in a short time our hands were awkward and blue with the cold. It was backbreaking too. My mother sat on a butter box, but we knelt or sat cross-legged. In a short time our muscles began to protest as we sorted the potatoes, throwing the bad ones into a container, which would be collected by a man to feed his pigs. It was one of those occasions that needed talk to make it bearable, and talk we did.

"It was good of you to give the kids a treat," my mother said, "but you'll need to put money away for yourself."

"Ah, sure, she's only a week in the place," my father laughed. "Give the child a chance."

I told them about the funeral and the "Watchword" and how impressive it had all been.

My father stood up to ease his back and said, "Maybe that was one of the Citizen Army men who died."

"Probably like the GPO in 1916," Ger grunted. "Sure, if all who claim to have been there were there, there would have been as many as in Henry Street on Christmas Eve."

"You like the job then?" my mother asked.

"It's very different," I tried to explain. "You see, they believe that everybody is equal, the worker and the boss. The boss puts in his money and runs the business, but the worker puts in his work. Without workers the place can't run. Not like in the Lodge. . ."

This was a sore point. When the owner died the estate was sold, and with it went our home and my father's job. They hadn't been bad people. They had tried to do their best for us but merely from a sense of duty. My father's world had fallen apart when he had to leave the Lodge. My mother held her cold blue hands under her armpits to ease the pain.

"All the same, what would we have done without the unions in 1913?" my mother asked. "That lock-out hit everyone, man, woman and child. That was the worst of times when nothing was to be had to feed your kids. When you've seen hunger, real hunger, when people would scavenge the dustbins of the well-off to get something to eat, you remember them that fed you. I will never forget standing as a child on that queue at the docks for the food parcels from the British miners. My father and the other men held up the wall of the pub and looked on. They said they were too proud to beg. With kids at home starving, I ask ye!"

She stood up to go inside and make some tea, nodding at me to go along with her.

"So you're a union woman," I said. I grinned as we put on the kettle and got the cups ready. "I never knew that."

She busied herself cutting soda bread. "I never worked long enough to be a real union woman, but I know enough to admire men like Connolly and Larkin. We need strong people to fight for those of us who are weak and who can't fight for ourselves."

She scraped margarine on the bread and covered over the deficiencies with the cheapie jam.

"I mean, who do we have to doff the cap to? The rent man, the ESB man, the doctor, the clergy, the Vincent de Paul man— just about everybody who has a glimmer of power? We had to do it all the time in the Lodge. I always had to look out the window in case the gentry were on the avenue before I could let a child out. Every time I got pregnant, there was all this tut-tutting from the ladies who thought even two kids was a bit 'over the top'.

"At the same time John Charles McQuaid was telling us we sinned if we didn't have a child a year. Women had miscarriage after miscarriage, and their health was the forfeit, and nobody gave a damn. I think it's good that you got a job that you feel matters," she said quietly, "but it won't be all plain sailing."

"I'd earn more once I was out of my time in Mandelberg's."

My mother stopped abruptly as she was about to bring out the tea to the yard on the tin box lid.

"You could and end up making raincoats for the rest of your life. Grow up, child. There has to be something better than that for at least one of us."

So we brought the tea out and stood and stretched aching bones, drank our tea and ate the soda bread, mainly to alleviate the coldness in our bones. Truthfully, the smell of rotting potatoes was very like the smell of decayed flesh, and it could easily turn your stomach if you let it.

But as my father said, "The job's got to be done if the plates are to be filled," and that was that.

CHAPTER EIGHT

"ME MA'S OFF again," Eileen said, and I stopped dead in the path, so that people behind jostled into us. We were walking home from mass on Sunday, a social sort of occasion when people chatted and nodded to one another.

"She's not!"

"She is so. She told Josephine last night."

Josephine was Eileen's eldest sister and walking-out with her own boy friend, so it must be true.

"When?"

"She said she'd be going on her holidays to Holles Street in the early spring again."

"God—that means. . ."

Eileen nodded. "Thirteen, unless it's twins, of course. Oh God, don't let it be twins!"

In Eileen's family there were already twelve children living in the box-like houses we all lived in, and there were already two sets of twins in the family.

"How'll you manage?"

"I don't know. They say children are God's treasures, but I wish he'd divide them up more evenly. And me ma is older now and it might be dangerous. God, if she were to die. . ."

"She won't die. Your ma's been through worse. You'll see."

This was cold comfort and I knew it. Eileen and I were best friends. So were her mother and my mother. Living as we did so close to one another, there were few secrets. Her mother included us in her care whenever my mother was in hospital. "I'll look after the kids, Peg, just like my own," she'd say. She did just that.

We had five kids in our family (three, a gap, then two), and we were overcrowded. Multiply that by three and you got an idea of what it was like in Eileen's home.

A big pot of stew put on the range early in the day to simmer away was doled out to those present at five in the evening. There'd be a pot of boiled spuds emptied out on to a big plate in the centre of the table. The bigger kids ate quickly, then the girls turned to feed the youngest, mashing up the potatoes in the gravy and spooning it into mouths opening like little birds. If anyone wasn't there in time, too bad! Eileen's family were always very punctual for meals.

When your plate was filled, you found a corner to sit in (chairs were only for grown-ups), and you ate as quickly as you could. Then you got a wedge of bread and jam out of an enormous pot of "mixed fruit", kind of yellowy in colour, and took that out to the street with you.

In our own house we sat down together. There were fewer of us and the food was a bit more varied, and there was time to talk to each other, but want was ever present with us too.

In Eileen's house it was taken for granted that the older girls looked after the younger kids. Before Eileen and I went out on a Saturday night, she first had to either bathe the younger children or iron the clothes for Sunday morning. It was called "Saturday night's splash for Sunday morning's dash."

"God, everywhere you turn in our house there's babies, or babies' things, or babies' smells, or babies crying, or babies puking. Me da's going round like a turkey cock!"

I looked at her, head down, hat in hand, walking beside me so straight and tall. Eileen was a real Irish colleen, slender, dark-haired and grey-eyed, with beautiful clear skin. She was the same age as me and she worked in a newsagent's. I touched her arm in sympathy.

"Roll on Galway," I said with a smile. We had plans to spend our very first holiday away from home in Galway. We planned to go by train, take our bikes and pedal around Connemara for a week. Our plans were gone over, changed and modified as Eileen picked out possible alternative places from the holiday ads in the newspapers she saw every day. There were a few problems, of course. We wouldn't be let go until we were eighteen, we had no bikes, and we had no money.

Eileen brightened up. "I saw this ad in the *Mail* for a place in Dungarvan. It sounded gorgeous. Where is Dungarvan?"

That night, as I was putting out the milk bottles, my mother came home from a walk with Eileen's mother. This was just a walk to "get a breath of fresh air".

The greatest social excess of the two mothers was an odd go at the first house in the local cinema when the seats were cheapest. They also attended the Monday night Novena in the Pro Cathedral, followed by a saunter around town looking at Clery's and Guiney's shop windows for bargains. That outing cost only the bus fare.

"Did you hear about Eileen's mother. . ." I started.

My mother held the cup of tea tightly in her hands to warm them and drank from it thirstily.

"I did," she said. "It's not for us to mind other people's business."

"But thirteen. . .! I mean. . ."

"If all Abbie's children had lived, there would have been eighteen," she said sombrely. "Each year for sixteen years that

woman has carried a child, sometimes two, in her womb. Sixteen bloody years! Don't try to tell me that's God's will, because
it's not! And when you think of those poor dead babies."

My mother sat warming herself by the dwindling heat of the
range, looking very sad. Then she stirred herself. "It's bed for
you, child," she said. "I'll put out the light." As I moved away I
quite distinctly heard her mutter something about a scissors,
and I knew exactly what she meant.

When I arrived into work on Monday, Jim was already in his
office, surrounded by books and papers, deeply immersed in
some kind of calculation.

"Good morning," he said. I asked if I might go for stamps to
the GPO. He waved me off with a smile, trying to hold his place
in a line of figures. I got out the money and the book and went
to buy the stamps in the GPO. Then I went into the shop on my
way back. Nellie was serving while Rosie was in deep conversation with a man at the back of the shop. Other men lounged
around reading newspapers, arguing about football, picking out
horses and smoking, but none of them was buying anything.

Nellie produced the milk. "Anything else?" she asked
smilingly.

"Just to pay my account up to last Friday," I said. "With the
funeral. . ." She looked across at Rosie with some concern. You
could see that Rosie had been crying; her eyes were red and
swollen. Was she related to the dead man? I had no idea. I produced my Petty Cash book and showed Nellie the entries. "I
think that's right."

She looked at the book, a little bemused. "Exactly," she
agreed. "That's it to a penny."

"Just sign there," I asked. "It's a receipt like, to show I've paid.
I have to show it to Jim Gilhooley this morning."

She did, still looking bemused. I put away the book in my

pocket and took up the milk, ready to go. The man who'd been talking to Rosie stepped forward, his hand out.

"I'm Billy McMullen," he said with that Belfast accent I remembered from the phone. "We spoke about the Burton's strike on the phone. All's well now?"

I murmured my name and we shook hands as I tried to sort things out in my mind. This was the general president of the union, the man who had been the leader amongst the paper clips, charged with bringing the ship safely to port. A sort of captain, I supposed, and I was one of his crew.

"Yes, thank you, all is well. I've got to go. Jim is doing his bookwork this morning, and I've to account for the petty cash to him. I mustn't keep him waiting."

With that I was gone, conscious of leaving a little silence behind me.

I made the tea and brought a cup in to Jim, carefully placing it so that it wouldn't damage his papers. Then I got my book, the stamps, the tin cash box with the money in it, and placed it before him.

"The balance is right to Friday. I've to take the six stamps out for Frances. I would need a post book to record the stamps in and out, wouldn't I?"

He looked at the book and the cash and initialled the book with due solemnity. "That's perfectly in order," he said with a hint of a smile. "Yes, a post book is indicated. Let's see what we have that's suitable?" He rummaged in the press behind him and drew out a stiff-covered copybook, perfectly new. "That's it, don't you think? Just give it its proper title and away you go.".

I was putting a sticker on the cover when I looked up and there was Terry, watching me with interest.

"God, you young ones have it really made. The way you churn

out all that stuff on those woody-woodpecker machines of yours."

"Sure, isn't that progress, Terry," I ventured, finishing the job and looking at my handiwork with some pride. "If old fellas like you had their way, we'd be back in the days of Dickens."

Terry puffed clouds of smoke up towards the ceiling. "How far forward have we come? We've left the quills behind, I'll grant you, but look down the passage outside, or down the docks, or on the building sites, or in the two-bit factories out there in the back, and what do you see?"

I looked at him uncertainly. "But surely it's better. . ." Then I thought of Abbie O'Dowd approaching her seventeenth pregnancy and what it meant for her and her family, and I wondered.

"What about the lock for the door? That's what you're here for, isn't it, Terry?"

"Women! Just when you're getting up a good head of steam in an argument, they change the subject. God, isn't that typical?" He tapped out the pipe and bent to have a look at the door of the press.

"I just want a decent-looking lock, put on straight, that's all I ask for, no more."

He took out a battered-looking tape measure from his pocket and waved it in the general direction of the door, never really touching it.

"That's measuring?" I was sceptical.

"We all have our special skills. That's mine. I know that door is exactly thirty inches high and that the crosspiece is at an angle which comes just there."

He put his finger on the outside of the door and then opened it and the crosspiece was just where he'd indicated. I looked at it, at first impressed.

"You made the door! You chancer, Terry!"

"Guilty, your ladyship, like everything else in this godforsaken hole."

With that Terry was gone. I put my head in Jim's door. "Is it all right if I go to pay back those stamps to Frances?"

Jim nodded, his mind still working on the filling in of what looked like a very complex set of documents. I picked up the stamps and went down the stairs and in the door at the side of the shop and stopped absolutely dumbfounded. I had walked into a dance hall! I looked around at the wooden sprung flooring, a stage, spotlights, seating around the walls and decorations, tired paper chains, half-deflated coloured balloons and tinselly gew-gaws.

There were about fifty people, men and women, sitting in small groups, who didn't look up as the big door clanged behind me. The group near me, men only, were playing poker. Another male group sat in the corner playing shove-halfpenny, while another group had a game that looked like dominoes. Another small group were clustered around a man who apparently had the result of a race. They were checking place names and prices.

A woman was knitting an Aran jacket, another was embroidering a tapestry of some kind, more were absorbed in newspapers or magazines, and others were just talking amicably together. Who on earth were these people?

"It's yourself! Come to visit the plebs, I suppose. Ah well, you're very welcome anyway." Frances appeared, her hand out in welcome. She saw my surprise and tucked her arm in mine and led me away.

"Everyone is surprised at first. These people are the casuals, the waiting staff for the functions like weddings and dinners, things like that. The hotels can only job our members; nobody works who is not a member. You see, the hotels ring us in the morning with a list of what they want, and the members come in here to wait to be called. Michael comes out with the list and calls the members' names, and then they're contracted to fill the function that night, wherever it is. It's a bit like a social club here; everybody knows everybody else. They sit here until noon. If their name isn't called by then, they go home and come back tomorrow. It's a whole way of life for them. It's not one I'd want, I have to say."

She led me down a narrow corridor to her office, introducing me here and there to people who shook my hand and welcomed me. There didn't seem to be any obvious distinction between staff and member. I looked over the shoulder of an elderly man with a big register like mine and saw that his had bent pages and drunken soldiers all over the page as against my more orderly, disciplined army of figures.

"Here we are," Frances said, leading me into a little cupboard of an office. She perched expertly on a high stool, with one leg tucked around its legs, and indicated I should do the same.

"The branch committee meeting is just ending," Frances said. "These people represent all the major hotels in the city. There's talk of a strike, God forgive them. I just hope it doesn't come to that." As people passed by they waved, nodded, winked or gave some sort of salutation to Frances, and she returned it.

"You have to remember that Liberty Hall was a hotel. This was the functions end. The big room out there was the ballroom. The whole place is a rabbit warren of rooms like this anyway. It's in an awful state, isn't it?"

I nodded. "It's the coal shed that really scares me," I admitted.

"Ah, the fires. Yes, well, I'm a cold creature. I have that electric fire on down there at me feet all the time. I'd never survive otherwise."

A woman passed behind us and paused, and then she came back.

"This is Peg O'Donnell. Peg, this is May, the new girl down with Jim Gilhooley. We're just getting acquainted."

Peg held out her hand and I took it and murmured some greeting. There was some stilted conversation, mainly about how Sadie was, a subject about which I knew little. When she moved on, Frances sighed and said, "She's is not one of my fans, but you must remember that Peg was actively involved in 1916 and all that. Frank Robbins goes on and on about that, but I really don't listen any more. It just goes over my head."

She touched my arm.

"You see, Peg sees me as the usurper, the one who's taking her place. Her problem is that nobody has time to listen to her any more. The members just want service; they don't give a fiddler's elbow who gives it."

I dug the six stamps out of my pocket. "I owe you them," I said. "I got more and I wouldn't want to mess up your post book."

She looked at me, obviously surprised. "What post book?"

It was my turn to look surprised. "To record the stamps in and out. The teacher in the Tech said. . . Anyway, the other thing I wanted to ask you is about running off stencils. Where's the Gestetner?"

"There," she said, pointing to a machine in the darkest corner of the passage. "The first time you use it give me a shout and I'll show you how. It's a bit eccentric and needs a firm hand. Listen, if you want to join me at lunchtime tomorrow, come in at one o'clock and we'll have a bite together. All right?"

I agreed with alacrity. There were so many questions I wanted to ask, and Frances seemed to have all the answers.

CHAPTER NINE

T ERRY WAS STANDING in the doorway, puffing away at his pipe and watching the passing traffic as I went out to the post box.

"Look at all I've done," I said. "Eleven letters, isn't that good?"

"Yeah, and that calls for eleven replies, eleven files to be updated. I tell you, we'll drown in a mass of totally unnecessary paper just to keep you young ones in your jobs."

After tea that evening, my mother sat the two youngest kids down in front of the range to read the comics they had accumulated from neighbours since the little lad's illness. They sat there as happy as Larry, checking on the adventures of Desperate Dan and Korky the Cat. My father set off on his bike for the plot, where he was hoping that he could do a deal to dig half of another man's plot for a share of the produce.

My mother indicated to the three of us to hang on for a while as there was something she wanted to talk to us about.

"Hurry up, Ma," Ger said. "I've to go. . ."

"This will only take a minute," she said. "I hate to have to tell you, but we have two problems: one is a biggie and the other less so. The biggie is that the rent's gone up since last week, and I don't know how I can pay it tomorrow."

"Bastards!" Ger said. "You'd think. . ."

"We've used more electricity and more fuel as well, so the bills are higher, and there's the cost of the doctor and the prescriptions. The chemist's giving me a bit of leniency, but I can't. . ."

"What about St Vincent de Paul?" Con asked.

"That ould bags," Ger growled. "He gives only to his cronies."

"Lads, please!" My mother was obviously very distressed. "I can't cut down on things any more, not with the young lad being sick. God, I'm so afraid of TB. That little Maher boy around the back, he went so quickly."

"Kevin is getting better," Con said. "You can see it in him."

My mother was still pursuing her own particular demon. "I don't like the sound of our little lad's cough, and he's still very weak."

Her eldest son, Tony, had died of diphtheria at the age of six, many years before. The scars still remained. The few times she talked about it she always said, "The child burned up in my arms and nothing could be done."

"Our main problem is we're spending more than we've got coming in," I said.

"Brilliant," Ger said. "That's bookkeeping theory for you. Can we deal with the practicalities for a minute?"

"It's plain and straight," my mother said. "Your father's job as a lorry driver won't pay more, and he's under pressure, and I don't want him worried. He does the very best he can for us. So it's up to us. I thought I could work a few nights cleaning and make a few bob, but I need to keep an eye on the little fellow. The bills are mounting and we've nothing to sell. Christmas is just down the road, and we can't let there be no Santa Claus at all."

Ger at sixteen was the eldest in the family and was working for the bus company as a messenger. We knew that he would be let go when he turned eighteen.

I was next at fifteen, and I was pretty sure my wages would stay static for the time being at least, but the pound I could give my mother was already eaten up by the additional expenses. My own main outlay was my bus fare. Was there any way I could cut that down?

Con at thirteen was still at school but got paid a few bob for delivering milk in our area for the milkman. That meant he met the milk float at the top of the avenue at half-seven in the morning and did the running while the milkman sat and smoked a cigarette or two and glanced over the morning paper as the horse ambled along at his own pace.

"That's the biggie," Con said. "Let's leave it aside for the moment. What's the smaller one?"

"The young lad's fourth birthday is tomorrow," my mother said, "and I've got nothing for him. We came damn near to losing him. I'd love to. . ."

"Get him red jelly. Sure, he loves that," Ger said. "I suppose a cake is out of the question?"

"I'll go early to the bakery for the bread," Con said, "and I'll ask that young one to throw in something fancy. I'd have more chance with her than with Scarey Mary.

The bread the rounds men returned to the local bakery after their day's work was sold as "stale bread" to those first in line. The shop girls filled a pillow-case, and sometimes you'd be lucky and get fancies: Vienna rolls, duck loaves and sometimes even a few cakes.

"I saw a little wooden train set in a shop window in Mary Street," Ger said. "It was in bits, a wheel or two off, and it needs painting. I'd get it for a few pence, I'm sure, and we could fix it up. Couldn't we, Con?"

Con nodded and, rooting in his trousers pocket, brought out a motley collection of bits and pieces, twine, a couple of hooks, an old brass army button, a multi-coloured marble, a few ciga-rette coupons and sevenpence. He pushed the money over towards my mother's hand.

"I'll get over the wall into the golf course and see if I can find a few golf balls to sell back to the caddy master," he said quietly.

Ger fished in his pockets and contributed one shilling and threepence. "I don't have travel expenses, and I don't have to dress myself up," he half apologised. "I wonder if there's any chance I'd get into the railway as a fireman when I'm eighteen. I'd be big enough, I think. I know the hours are desperate, but the money. . ."

My mother sighed, hands up hiding her face. "God, I hate this," she said. "Why do we always have to. . ."

"Right," Con interrupted. "Will you get the train set, Ger? I'll look out a bit of paint."

"Now back to the biggie," Ger said. "For Christmas, the young lad would love one of those Black Bob storybooks. You know, the one about the sheepdog? There are loads of really good books going for half nothing after the fire in that bookshop, and some of them are hardly damaged at all." Having a split shift meant Ger had loads of time to put in walking around town.

"Your Aunt Jess is getting a doll for Kate for Christmas," my mother said. "She's knitting the clothes from one of those *Woman's Own* patterns, a full set of clothes, but I think she's find-ing it hard going. Knitting is really not her thing."

We all had to smile at that. Aunt Jess and knitting were not natural soulmates. I'd been thinking hard as the talk went on. I could cut my lunch, just bring in a slice of bread. There was loads of tea and so on in the office. I got my purse and put two shillings down on the table.

"There you go, Ma; can we get by for the rest of the week?" My mother nodded, her hand still covering her mouth. "Not a word to your father about this. I don't want him worried. You understand?" We nodded and went our separate ways, all too aware of how thin the line was between survival and going under.

When I got home from work next day, the birthday festivities were well under way. The young lad was sitting between Kate and Con on the wooden bench my father had made and was looking with wonder as my mother upended the jelly mould and the red jelly, in the shape of a castle, slid out, slithery and trembly.

My father took his place at the head of the table and solemnly shook the little lad's hand, wished him a Happy Birthday and gave him a chocolate bar.

"He's not the 'little lad' any more," Kate said out of the blue. "He's Kevin and he's four. He'll be going to school soon. We'll have to learn to call him Kevin now he's four."

We all looked at Kate, totally surprised. She herself was all of five and in low babies class at school.

"Kate's right," my father said, a bit sadly. "Kevin's not a baby any more. So from today 'the little lad' is banned as a name. How's that, Kevin?"

My mother brought in plates of sausage and mash, Kevin's favourite, and we started to eat, Kevin's eyes still on the jelly. He was fascinated at the way it shook and wobbled once a spoon was put into it. Then my mother gave Con the nod, and he put out the light. My mother carried in a cake with four lit candles on it, and we all sang "Happy Birthday". It was only a Swiss roll, but the candles made it look festive. Kevin blew out the candles and we all told him to wish. His wish was simple: "To be able to go out and play."

Ger reached under his chair and produced a brown paper parcel bound with twine. "We got this specially for you so you can play with it inside in the warmness. When the weather picks up, you'll be able to take it outside. I bet you can never guess what we have for your birthday."

Thumb in mouth, Kevin lapsed into silence, his eyes on the parcel. My father cut the twine and began to open it slowly. Kevin wriggled across to sit on his knee and watch the gradual unfolding of the paper, almost not daring to breathe. When the red, blue and yellow little wooden train sat on the table, he chortled with delight, barely able to believe it was his.

"Choo-choo," my father went, guiding the little train around cups and plates. "Imagine that, you've got your very own little engine and carriage. There's where the driver stands, and he looks out that window to see where he's going, and the passengers all sit in the carriages. . ."

"And they have lemonade," Kate said. "'Cause they're on their holidays."

My father put Kevin down on the floor to play with the train, and then Kevin was joined by Kate. "You did well, boys," my father said. "You'd never guess the bits that were missing. It looks brand new."

Ger was mightily pleased with his purchase.

"The paint dried in time." Con was relieved. "I got up in the night to see how it was doing," he confessed.

We looked at the two children on the floor, coupling and uncoupling the little carriage, reversing, drawing up to a station made of a book, the toy as real to them as if we'd got it from the biggest store in town.

"That worked out well," Con said. "But, God, next time, Ma, give us a bit of advance warning!"

CHAPTER TEN

THAT NIGHT, IN bed, as the wind scoured the street outside and the rain lashed against the window, I went back over the day's happenings in my mind.

Both Kate and Kevin were no longer babies. They were inseparable now, but they would go to school together at first and then be separated. He would have go to the boys' school and she to the girls'. Then the struggle for jobs would start.

Of our family, I probably had the most secure job, unless, of course, I let the fires go out again! My father's job, drawing sand by lorry down the Embankment to the building sites, ceased when the weather got really bad or whenever there was a glut of sand, or at the whim of the gaffer. Ger's job would end when he was eighteen. There was nothing in prospect for him. Con, what would he get? A factory job loading stuff if he was lucky.

Our problem was that as we got older we needed more space, clothes, food, everything, and it looked as if we'd never have enough to meet our needs. Surely that was wrong. The end of the war had been celebrated by everyone, an end of bombing, of massive shelling, of the concentration camp atrocities, of all the horror that is part to war. In Ireland now we were suffering because of the peace. There was less work, more people idle, economic stagnation, a triumphalist Church and a compliant government.

It seemed to me as though some ideals still lived on in Liberty Hall, although a bit muted, a bit down at heel. I wondered, where were the women? Women like my mother who had her own opinions but seemed never to be listened to? Women like my friends who worked on piece rates till they dropped just to earn a bit above the basic rate? The health issue made obvious by Abbie's seventeenth pregnancy? Was women's health ever talked about?

Surely men like Jim Gilhooley or Frank Robbins had some answers.

Shortly after I got into work that morning, a woman had arrived at the counter looking for me. Sadie had looked a bit askance at that.

"There she is. You had better make it snappy, she's got plenty of work to do," she'd growled, looking at me from under her glasses.

The woman said, "I'm Frances Lambert's sister. She won't be in today. She's sick. She'll be in touch." Then she scurried out.

"What's this? Are you meeting that young rossie?" Sadie asked.

"She was going to show me how to run off circulars on the machine down there at lunchtime." I was being economical with the truth at best, but she let it pass without further comment.

Now I wondered about Frances. Well, maybe she thought I wasn't up to her standards in clothes, hairdo, make-up, jewellery, the lot. It was true I was a bit of an in-between. Most of my clothes still had the schoolgirl look about them, that green gabardine coat, for instance. My shoes were scuffed. My hair was trimmed at the ends with just a hairclip holding it from my face. Frances seemed the height of glamour to me. Maybe I wasn't in her class.

CHAPTER ELEVEN

As I TRUDGED slowly up the stairs in Eden Quay next morning, I heard my name called softly from behind. I turned and it was Paddy McLoughlin.

"Hold on a minute there," he whispered, his hand holding his scarf up to his face. "Would you ever slow up?"

"Anyone inside?" he asked, nodding his head towards our door.

"No. They're away. Why?"

"Have you a first-aid box in there?"

I remembered seeing a box with a first-aid cross on it. "Yes. I don't know what's in it though."

"I need a bit of help." He held my arm and whispered in my ear. "I don't want the Bull to know."

I unlocked the office door, and he sat down rather suddenly in one of the chairs. I realised that the red of the scarf was congealing blood.

"What happened?" I asked. "Get your coat off, and I'll get a towel."

"I had a row about union money on the site, an inter-union squabble. Some bastard landed a lucky punch, but I gave as good as I got."

He had a cut over his eyebrow with the blood still seeping out, an eye that was swollen and closing fast, an egg-sized bruise on his cheekbone and a split lip. He was also bleeding from his mouth, and his knuckles were raw and deeply grazed.

"You need to go to hospital, Paddy. A few stitches maybe. . ."

"Fuck that! No way." I had never heard Paddy swear before, and it made me realise the extent of his problem.

"All right. I'll do what I can."

I dipped my handkerchief in some cold water and wiped away the blood, checking inside his mouth to see where the blood was coming from.

"I've a tooth loose, I think," he spluttered. "I bit my tongue too. Oh my God, I'll never live this down."

I poured some hot water into a bowl, threw a generous amount of disinfectant in and began cleaning out the wounds.

"Jesus! Take it easy!" he pleaded. "That hurts!"

I dried the eyebrow cut and squeezed some antiseptic jelly on and then applied a dressing

"I can't do anything for inside your mouth; it'll have to heal itself. You won't be eating anything solid for a while."

Paddy was sitting, head in hands, looking very sorry for himself. I made tea, handed him a mug with two aspirin, and took his scarf to the toilet to rinse out the bloodstains. When I got back he was looking at himself in the mirror.

"I look like I went ten rounds with Joe Louis," he groaned. "God, I'll never hear the end of it from Tommy."

"But why?"

"Well, since the split, when the Workers' Union of Ireland went off to do their own thing, there's been a lot of inter-union rivalry. I was collecting the union dues from my men on the site when this bastard down-faced me. One word borrowed another, and in the heel of the hunt he gives me the shoulder. You know, a push. Then he said to me, 'So what are you going to do about it, brother?' I pushed back, he threw an uppercut, and it went downhill from there."

Paddy sat by the fire drinking his tea as I went on with my work. He suddenly jumped up, spilling the tea. "God, my bike! I left it down at the door, it's probably been robbed!"

Luckily the bike was still there, and between us we hauled it up the stairs where he examined it closely before locking it beside the garden shed.

"That bike is union property," Paddy said. "Imagine having to go to head office and say, 'Sorry, I lost your ould bike, and I don't know where it is.' Sure, I'd have to make a report on how I left it downstairs in Eden Quay and not under Terry's eagle eye. In triplicate probably."

He explained that he left home around half-seven each morning on his bike to tour building sites on the south side of the city. He collected union money, did membership card checks, took in new members, vetted the safety of scaffolding and so on, and got from the men some idea of the duration of the work and where possible new sites might open.

"The shovels in the office?" I hesitated to ask.

"Oh yes, the shovels. Well, a labourer must have a shovel or he can't be jobbed. When a site closes down and they're all laid off, most have a formidable thirst. It goes with the job. There's a huge temptation to pledge the shovel in the pawnshop to get more money for drink while they wait for a new site to open. If the men can't raise the money to redeem the shovel, they can't start on the job without it. So we try to have them leave them with us."

"It's a hard ould life, Paddy."

"For me? Sure, they think I have it soft. For them, well, it's hard wherever you are, on the docks, on the sites, in the mines, on the ships. For the labourers, it's often the bad weather, the cold seeps into you, and the uncertainty. They know they will be laid off when the weather gets bad. All too often they are laid off in August just before they're due to be paid holiday pay. It's like anywhere else: there's good employers and there's rogue employers, and too damn many go-by-the-wall chancers who'd take a penny off a blind man."

When he felt a little better, Paddy went off to his own office, and I was left thinking over what he'd said.

Jim came in and asked me to check some figures with him. He called out figures from a list, and I checked them from a printed sheet.

"You don't know what it is, do you?" he asked.

I shook my head.

"You see, there's a legal minimum rate of wages in the trade. Employers must pay at least that, although some pay more. The place I organised this morning is paying about 20 per cent below the legal minimum. That's what we were doing just now, checking one against the other.

"The little weasel of an employer just grinned and threw shapes and did a Pontius Pilate act when I put my suspicions at him. He knew nothing, had heard nothing, had seen nothing about any legal minimum rate. The number of times he called God to witness the truth of what he said, he should have been struck down dead!"

"What happens now?"

"We will put in a claim for our members for what's due to them, and we will report it to the Department of Industry and Commerce. They may, or may not, send an inspector to check. There are too few inspectors and too many possible culprits. In the meantime, the little weasel will probably do a runner to escape having to pay out."

"What can you do?"

He shrugged his shoulders. "A sit-in, maybe, is all we can do. It's hard to say. It depends largely on the members. Some will drift away, those who don't have much to lose. Women now, they tend to be the most tenacious in cases like this. For them it's often a case of 'the law says, do as the law says'. Men tend to get hung up in the nitty-gritty. I find that women tend to look for solutions."

Jim took up the message jotter. "So, you had a quiet morning?" he said.

I looked at him in surprise.

"Only a few messages," he smiled.

"Well, I played Florence Nighingale for Paddy McLoughlin. He was in a fight on a building site."

"Ye're joking! Is he all right? Not badly hurt?"

"He has cuts and bruises and an impressive shiner. He's a bit self-conscious about it, and he doesn't want Tommy to know. Inter-union rivalry he said it was. What's that?"

"Well, James Connolly founded the Irish Transport and General Workers' Union and he was our leader. He was executed by the British after the 1916 Rising, and James Larkin then became the leader. James Larkin went to America, and in his absence changes occurred in our union. I won't go into all the details; they are very complex. The row brought about another union, the Workers' Union of Ireland. Both unions represent workers in much the same employments, and there's little love lost between the two. You saw at Tom's funeral how the Starry Plough, our flag, was guarded. It's largely ceremonial now, but there was a time when it wasn't.

"Personally, I believe the losers in inter-union conflicts are the workers both unions represent. We lose too much time and effort in justifying our position and vilifying the other side. Of course, the employers can sit back smugly and smile at our antics. Now, Frank Robbins wouldn't share my sentiments."

"So he. . ."

"Well, you'll have to ask Frank about that. Frank's always been his own man, and he wouldn't thank me for interpreting what his views might be."

CHAPTER TWELVE

"SHIT!" SAID THE postman as he leaned his bike up against the wall beside our door on Eden Quay. Coming behind him, head down in the rain, my milk and biscuits balanced precariously, I bumped into him. His very full postbag slid sideways, its contents plopping down on the wet pavement. I grabbed the handlebars with my one free hand and held the bike steady as he groped for his wet and grubby letters.

"Shit, shit, shit!" He held the envelopes up, wet, dirty and with the ink already smudging. He groped ineffectively for a handkerchief beneath his rain gear to wipe them clean.

"I'll take these in for you if you want."

"That fucking little bastard in the front hall should be taken to the river and dumped like you'd dump a dead dog. Let the fishes do a job on him, the stuttering little bastard!"

I gathered, through the swearing, that Terry had refused delivery of a parcel for Frank Robbins on the grounds that it was addressed to the ITGWU at Eden Quay and not at Beresford Place. Our post wasn't usually delivered to Eden Quay because our letterbox was subject to vandalism, so the postman had a legitimate grievance.

"Sorry about that," I muttered, wondering why I'd to apologise for Terry's vagaries. "Sure, I'll take it in. Frank Robbins works in the office just beside me."

"They should do something about that little viper," he muttered, holding out the book for me to sign. "Jesus, and he's supposed to speak for the union. He has no manners whatsoever. That man wouldn't know the word if it came up behind him and bit the arse off him!"

I took the post and knocked on the Theatre and Cinema Branch door. Somebody called out, "Come in," and I entered with some curiosity. This office was at the front of the building, with windows opening on to Eden Quay. There was a youngish man talking on the phone. He cocked an eyebrow enquiringly and I held out the parcel.

"In there," he mouthed.

Frank was sitting at a vast littered desk. He was in shirtsleeves with red braces. "So, you got around to visiting us," he smiled, putting on his jacket and straightening his tie. "About time too."

"I met the postman. Terry wouldn't take it at the front door, and his bag fell to the ground and his post got all wet."

"That Terry is an obstinate little weasel," Frank said, checking the stamps and the return address. "M'm, I was expecting this. It was good of you to bring it over."

I turned to leave. "Hold on a moment there," he said. "How are things going with you?"

"It's OK, I think."

"Different from school?"

"Oh yes. There everything is always the same. Here, well, you never know what'll happen."

I watched as Frank took up the package and forced the well-secured parcel apart with his bare hands. Inside were magazines with international union logos on the masthead, or at least so I deduced from the bits I could read.

I looked around the office. On the walls behind Frank's desk were photographs. They showed Frank with actors, film stars, politicians and clerics. It was very impressive. The same flags as ours stood in the corner. His branch banner showed two outline faces, one crying and one smiling. Was that the symbol for actors, I wondered.

Over the mantelpiece hung a picture of the same woman I'd seen in Jim's office. She was tall, regal and dressed in a beautiful ball gown. I got up to have a closer look.

"Are you interested in the Countess?" Frank asked.

"Yes. There is a smaller picture of the same woman in Jim's office. Who is she?"

Frank sat back. "God, do they teach you anything at all about history in school?" he growled.

"We went up as far as Easter Week, the GPO and all that stuff. We mostly learned about the Wild Geese really, I think."

"Well, the woman is Constance Gore-Booth. She lived on an estate called Lissadell in Sligo. I suppose she was a typical Anglo-Irishwoman. She excelled at hunting, shooting, fishing, dancing, theatricals, art and music. She married a Polish count, that's where the Countess bit comes in. Her married name is Countess Markievicz. In 1913 in the Great Dublin Lock-out, when the bosses tried to break our union, Madame came into our lives. She worked in the soup kitchen here in Liberty Hall.

"I'll never forget the first time I saw her as a young lad. She was tall, slender, with a back as straight as a die, and she moved quickly, gracefully, smoothly. You can get some idea of her beauty from the picture. In real life, with her eyes lit up, face animated, laughing, sharing something precious with you, she had that way with her. She would put her hand on your shoulder, with her head tilted to one side, those dark eyes willing you to explain something to her.

"I became one of her Fianna boys, like many another young lad living in the tenements, where poverty, illness, hunger and the greyness of a life lived mainly on the street was commonplace. Then she came with talk of the Fianna, Finn McCool, Oisín, the Red Branch Knights—an Irish glorious past that we knew nothing about. It was like a light, a glorious wonderful light, she brought into our lives. We would have gladly died for her, every man jack of us."

"And. . ." I breathed.

"When Easter Week came I followed her out to her assigned position in Stephen's Green as a sergeant of the Citizen Army. Madame was my lieutenant. After the Rising she waited in a nearby cell as the leaders were shot day after day, Pearse, McDonagh, the lot. When Connolly—our leader. . ."

Frank looked bleakly out the window. "So that was that. 'A terrible beauty was born,' somebody said about the Rising. It's to our eternal disgrace that we allowed 'Sinn Féin' to become 'Mé Féin' in the years that followed."

"And the Countess?"

"Madame, that's what we always called her. Mind you, she had her faults, nobody's perfect. That Anglo-Irish accent. And the big words. She could be so obstinate! But she was our Madame; there is nobody like her, nor will there ever be."

"But, Mr Robbins, that's over thirty years ago. You still feel. . ."

"I'll just say this, no more. If Madame stood here this day and asked me to walk across burning coals in my bare feet, the only question I'd ask is, 'Will I do it now, Madame?'"

Frank turned away and I got up to go, knowing this discussion was over.

I sat back at my desk, my mind still working out what Frank had said. The Countess. . .

Frances Lambert put her face around the door.

"Still interested in a bite to eat? Lil told you I couldn't make it the last time?"

She came in, make-up glowing, hairdo the height of fashion, clothes too. I looked at her silently.

"Sulking, are we?" she laughed. She perched on the corner of my desk. "No need to, sulk, I mean. I've a bad chest. This damp weather is my worst time. I have to take to the bed, but sure who wants to hear somebody moaning? I don't usually say anything about it. You understand?"

I nodded.

"So you'll come in at one?"

"All right.

With a nod and a wink she was gone, and I could hear her high heels do their drumbeat across the room outside.

Jim stood warming himself in front of the fire. "Christmas is around the corner," he said. "Are either of you doing anything special?"

Sadie said something about her plans, but I knew ours were likely to hit a real snag. My father's job was not going well. The sand lorries were like loaded ants on the Embankment Road. They came down heavily loaded on schedule and toiled up empty. My father felt there was not enough maintenance work done on them, particularly on the brakes. The owners were only interested in getting the sand down, not in the safety element, even though the men themselves were afraid that someday someone would get killed. Would the job last till Christmas? I knew my mother had grave doubts.

Jim was speaking and I pricked up my ears. "We'll take in the collectors' books from next week. The registers will be here from the printers this week. I'll do the factory outline first thing so that we can begin to write out the new registers."

"What? We've to write new registers by Christmas? Sure that's impossible." The words burst from my lips without thought. "I mean. . ."

"M'm. It's onerous, that's true, but we manage to do it every year somehow. This year in you we've an extra pair of hands." Jim teetered on his heels, hands in trousers pockets.

I looked at him aghast. "But. . ."

"We can't do it till a few weeks before Christmas because of the way people come and go in jobs. So we write in the names from the shop steward's book into the new register with this year's number. Then we write a new shop steward's book with the new numbers. You see, this year's numbers lapse with the end of the current year, and from January everyone has to have a new number. You can't have the two sets of numbers mingling."

I thought of the three thousand or so names in the registers and winced.

"It won't be all that bad," Jim laughed. "We'll all do our share, and I'll get a couple of members to give us a dig out. It'll mean a bit of working late though. The union doesn't pay overtime, but we'll organise time off instead. All right?"

I nodded. Surely there must be a better system. . .

Jim looked at the clock. "Off you go to your lunch now. See you later."

Clutching the brawn sandwich in its brown paper bag that I'd stuffed into my pocket before leaving the house, I clattered down the stairs and into the Hotel Branch. I heard Frances yelling and I followed the sound of her voice past the small groups of casuals waiting for work. Most nodded or smiled, apparently recognising me from my last visit. Frances led me past her office.

"We'll get a bit of peace in here," she said, slamming the door of the office behind her.

We were in a branch secretary's office with a very ornate desk and chair, a soft upholstered visitor's chair, a coffee table covered with newspapers and magazines, the tops of the filing cabinets littered with photographs of cabinet ministers, diplomats and the archbishop. A side table was covered with white butcher's paper. Frances pulled the paper aside with a flourish.

"*Voila!*" she said. "What about that?"

My jaw dropped in amazement. There were silver trays of food, little biscuity things covered with fillings, many I couldn't recognise at all. And the sandwiches, little three-cornered, mouth-size, crust-less pieces. Glasses were filled with desserts, ice cream, mousse, strawberries and cream, things I'd never seen before.

"Let's waste no time!" Frances laughed. "I filled the kettle already so I'll just plug it in." I watched with envy, thinking of the tediousness of the way we boiled our kettle on the open fire.

"But why. . ."

"Our chefs have a competition. They must provide a full meal within a certain time. The idea is that the winners go to represent Ireland in the international competition. The judging panel sat here this morning and the hotel chefs supplied their meal. So this is what was left over. I thought it'd make a change from chips."

I thought of my brawn sandwich and smiled. Frances opened the door of a press and drew out a very ornate silver salver. "This is what they won. I've to get the winning chef's name and his hotel etched on it. It's nice, isn't it? That's smoked salmon, try a bit? That's paté, and that's anchovy. Over there's smoked eel. Or would you like to try a bit of caviar?"

Then on to the desserts, a spoonful of this, a little glass of that, a taste of something else. "Sorry there's no booze," Frances apologised. "A little drop of wine would go well with this. But your man, he keeps all alcohol under lock and key. Sure you'd have to here. You know how it is."

When it was time to go back to work, Frances drew out a bag and began to put things into it. "This is for you to bring home. It'll give the kids a bit of a treat."

She then went out to the kitchen and came back with a container, which she thrust into my hands. Inside was a spun sugar confection, a circus scene with ponies, clowns, a trapeze artist, lions and tigers, and in the centre an iced pool with seals, polar bears, penguins and a snowman. I looked at her with amazement.

"Ask Nellie to keep it in the freezer till you go home. That was the biggie. God knows how long it took to make that scene, and it seems a shame to just let it melt."

"Thanks," I muttered. "God, the two little ones will love that. And it's so hard at Christmas."

That night when I got home, I opened the bag amidst great wonder and excitement as my family tried out the various canapés and sandwiches, but the pièce de résistance was undoubtedly the circus scene. It was lovely to see the wonder on the kids' faces as the spun sugar circus came to our house.

CHAPTER THIRTEEN

ABBIE O'DOWD'S SEVENTEENTH pregnancy wasn't going well. She'd taken weak at the shops, and the local coalman had driven her to our door in his ramshackle, clanky ould van with the coal sacks balanced precariously at the back.

"I don't know. . . Maybe it's the hospital she needs," he'd confided to my mother. "It doesn't look right to me."

With eleven of his own kids at home, he was a bit of an authority on the subject and deserved to be listened to, unlike most men.

In general there was no link between men and women about "women's problems". Men talked about work, or the lack of it, or football, the horses, politics, the weather, engines—whatever subject was their particular fancy. Women dealt with the practicalities of life, like eking out whatever money they got, paying the bills, looking after their family's health, making sure their children went to school, and dealing, often on their own, with the "women's problems" that were part and parcel of their lives.

Abbie lay on my parents' bed looking a bit like a stranded whale. She was enormous already, and strong rumours of the possibility of another set of twins were already circulating. My mother did the best she could, but looking at Abbie's swollen ankles, hands and red flushed face, she'd sent Con for Mrs Jennings for her advice.

Mrs Jennings was the wise woman in our locality. She dealt with births, deaths and illnesses, deferring to the medics when circumstances dictated. She was always trusted, as the doctors in the clinics seldom were. She cleaned up, laid-out, lanced boils, applied poultices, bandaged cuts and sores, gave advice and watched intently whatever went on around her. She knew more about us all individually than anyone ever dreamt.

Mrs Jennings looked Abbie straight in the eye. "It's not going right, Abbie. You know that yourself."

"Is it the babby?" Abbie asked fearfully.

"It's your womb, all those other births. . .The babby's badly placed and it needs help."

"Can you. . .?"

"No. This is a hospital job. The swelling and the shortness of breath means you need help, Abbie, and quickly if you're to save the babby."

"But my other babbies! What'll happen them? Oh my God, the two little ones! I can't leave them!"

Mrs Jennings held Abbie's red, swollen hands in hers and spoke gently. "You've no choice, Abbie. I know it's not easy. This pregnancy is putting an awful strain on your body. It can't cope, and the little babby is being poisoned by the toxins your body can't get rid of. You've no choice, Abbie."

Abbie turned her face into the pillow and cried bitterly. Mrs Jennings silently went on stroking her hand, and my mother shooed me out of the room.

"You'll hit that hurdle soon enough," she said bitterly. "The poor woman, my heart goes out to her. Her insides are being torn apart, and the hospital will treat her like a prize specimen. Those students will treat her like she was a picture in some medical book—'Now, mother, tell me. . .' And that husband of hers is going around like a bloody turkey cock!"

My mother banged down the crockery she was drying so hard I thought it would break. Her own experience with childbearing hadn't been the best. The public maternity nurse on Con's confinement had carried childbed fever to many of her patients without knowing it. After the birth my mother had been taken to Cork Street Fever Hospital, where she got over that particular illness but succumbed to a succession of other fevers.

She had been lucky enough to survive a truly terrible ordeal over a twelve-month hospital stay. After that long period of bed confinement, she'd had to learn to walk again. All the time she'd fretted for her baby, Con, who was growing up in the care of a relative, and for us—Ger and myself—who wouldn't know our mother when we saw her again. My mother's feelings about the medical profession were a bit jaundiced to say the least.

Abbie was taken from our house by ambulance, with Josephine and my mother sitting with her. Mrs Jennings stood in the doorway to see them off.

"Now, let's see how we stand," she said to our neighbours as she settled her scarf back around her neck after the ambulance had turned the corner. "I can take one of the twins. May Carroll, I'm sure, can take one too. But we've got to make sure the older ones are cared for. Let's see. . ."

"Eileen can come to us," I said quickly. "I know my mother won't mind."

Mrs Jennings looked at me, one eyebrow raised questioningly. "But in the circumstances. . .?"

I knew she knew how tight our budget was, but I was quite sure.

"Yes, Eileen should come to us. I'll run around now and tell her. Sure, she'll be very upset about her mother."

"Yes, child, I'm sure she will be. More so than her father maybe. I've asked Pauline in the post office to give him a ring at work. Signs on it, he'll ask who'll get him his dinner."

CHAPTER FOURTEEN

MY FATHER'S JOB ended the day after we started writing the new registers. By now I knew how to take in the members' money from the shop stewards and knew most of them, at least by name. Mostly they came in over the weekend, and they were easy to get on with, with the usual few exceptions.

They collected the money after the company had paid the wages, so what we got consisted of a lot of small coins, pennies, even halfpennies, threepenny pieces, sixpences and shillings, with a few notes. The shop stewards mostly took their duties very seriously. They were accountable to us but also to their members, in case they suspected that the shop stewards were pocketing some of the dues. So our receipt at the back of the book was very important. It had to be shown to some sceptics on the work floor to keep suspicions at bay.

They were paid commission on what they paid in, ten per cent of what was receipted at the back of the book. This too was a big thing for many. They tended to let it run till the holidays or a birthday or First Communion, when it'd make all the difference.

For me, taking in the money, it seemed at first impossible to get things balanced properly. I had to add up the amount written in the book. I then had to check that the cash corresponded and sign the receipt, hoping to God they weren't going to ask for their commission. That wasn't from any lack of willingness on my part, but it added up to more bookwork and more calculations against which I had to balance my cash at the end of the day.

It seemed endless, that counting of coins into little bags, rubber-banding them, checking the notes and hoping to God the lot would tally at the end of it all. Then next day going with arms trailing like a gorilla with the weight of it to the bank to lodge the money and bring Jim back the receipt.

Of course, we had our share of chancers, people who'd swear a hole through an iron pot that when they looked at it last their money was exactly right and calling on God to witness it. We also had our share of incompetents who just never knew what was in the little drawstring bag run up by a machinist to hold the union money. If they were short you marked the receipt short, and, of course, that'd draw some pretty pointed comments when it was revealed on the work floor.

To write the new registers, we retained certain shop stewards' books. Some were a bit wary about that; without the book they'd no way of showing they hadn't done a Danny with the money. We wrote the names and numbers into the new registers to Jim's formula. We then completed the new shop stewards' books for the New Year and posted out the old books or delivered them if they were city centre.

We kept a list of what was to be done pinned to the wall, and as we finished our factories we ticked them off, so we could see the picture emerge as to whether or not we would meet the deadline of the New Year. It seemed to me to be an impossible task, but Jim was always optimistic.

To add to the burden, Jim had to get in all outstanding contributions before the end of the year. That was a head office edict. If we didn't have all outstanding cash in, we'd lose financial membership, which was linked to our status as a branch. I didn't understand all of that, but it seemed to mean that Jim and Sadie were dashing around like headless chickens just when they were needed most in the office.

And needed they were. It seemed an odd thing, but coming up to Christmas three factories folded. The workers left work on the Friday in the normal way, and when they came in on Monday there was nothing left but the machines. All the cloth, trimmings, finished work, everything was gone, and after lunch men came and repossessed the machines for the hire purchase company. The members were out of work on the brink of Christmas, their employers couldn't be found, and, of course, nobody was hiring at that time of year, January being a slack time in the trade anyway.

I said as much to Paddy McLoughlin.

"Don't be daft," he responded. "It's the same as our lot in the building trade. The employers won't pay the bank holiday money, so they leg it. They think, why should they pay for people lolling at home doing nothing? That's how they see it. I know what I'd do with them, and it wouldn't be pleasant!"

At home things weren't going well. There'd been dissension in my father's job about the safety of the lorries, and the employer just employed other drivers who'd raise no questions. He had let the rest, including my father, go.

Ger had got a few extra bob by offering to help his old paper round employer do the sorting of the periodicals. She'd developed a bad back and was glad to have him come in on particular mornings at half-six to sort out the periodicals and magazines for the lads doing their routes.

Con went to the local golf course after school three evenings a week and fished in the water for golf balls to sell back to the caddy master. He was a canny negotiator, knowing there was merit in holding back his produce until the man was going mad to get golf balls, which he, in turn, would sell back to the members as new or semi-new.

My mother wanted to go out to work herself, but with my father as depressed as he was and the extra work Abbie's stay in hospital involved, she couldn't do it. It was strange to go to work and see my father still at home and come back and he'd be still there, sitting in his chair beside the range, scanning the newspapers that helpful neighbours supplied, to see could he get work.

He no longer read to us. We'd gone through *David Copperfield* so many times that we were on first name terms with all the Dickens characters. He no longer sang about the house, even the John McCormack songs he loved. He sat within a world of his own, surrounded by his own feelings of inadequacy, his inability to secure his family's future and his self-doubts, and nobody, not even my mother, could reach him.

Eventually he managed to be taken on the panel of temporary postmen for Christmas. That meant he walked to the sub-post office to which he was allotted at half-six and did four rounds of his allotted route per day. That marked quite a marathon in walking terms in itself. He also had to carry a heavy bag, and for a middle-aged countryman who never found walking on Dublin's pavements easy, it was really hard going.

I saw him come in at the end of the day, and even the laces of his boots would be bloodied. My mother would have a basin of water ready, and he'd bathe his feet, the water gradually turning red from the blisters on blisters that covered his feet. She'd dress the blisters as best she could, give him a clean pair of socks to put on because his swollen feet, once out of the boots, wouldn't go back in. Then she'd hand him his tea at the fire to avoid him having to stand. And, in no time, he'd be asleep, absolutely exhausted. My mother hated to have to call him for the next stint and watch him walk away stiffly, trying not to show his agony in his face.

Her friend Abbie, too, was going through a bad time. The doctors in the maternity hospital had been appalled at her state of health, and she lay in bed festooned with tubes and drips and pined after her children. My mother was right about the seventeen pregnancies being a wonder. Abbie confided to her, "I can't shut my eyes for five minutes but there's some eejit with a white coat and stethoscope looking at me sayng, 'Your seventeenth pregnancy, I don't believe it.' Jesus, you'd think they'd change the tune some day."

Eileen was like a ghost in our house, only waiting for a chance to go home. She missed her ma, that's for sure! But she also missed the noise, the excitement and the crowdedness of her own home. Ours was far too quiet, too staid, too orderly for her.

"Will me ma get home for Christmas?" was her theme song. My mother said she thought she would and that it would be nice if Josephine and herself got things ready in anticipation, knowing Abbie would need to keep off her feet over the next weeks. Eileen and Josephine entered into the spirit of this wholeheartedly, fixing a daybed in the kitchen where Abbie'd see everything that was going on. My mother looked a bit concerned about that but kept her thoughts to herself.

Christmas was almost upon us when Jim Gilhooley gave me a bit of a start by calling me into his office and closing the door behind me. I waited with some apprehension. Jim stood in front of the fireplace warming himself and said nothing for a moment.

"Things are difficult at home?" he said then, very gently. "Mind, I'm not probing, but if they are, maybe there's something I can do to help out. All of us hit our hard times some time in our lives. And a hand is sometimes needed."

I sat, head down, wringing my hands in my lap. "It's my father, his job is gone. He's on the Christmas post. His feet. . . it's awful!"

"M'm." Jim rocked on his heels, hands in trousers pockets. "Methylated spirits, that helps harden the feet. Just put a drop in the water. I'll get a bottle in the chemist's when I'm coming back and you can bring it home. It's worth a try anyway.

"Now, about paying you on Fridays. That's a bad idea, I think. Consumer goods go up in price at the weekend. That's statistically proven. If we were to change our pay day from Friday to Thursday, would that be inconvenient to you?"

I sat, mouth wide open in astonishment. "Thursday?" I spluttered. "Pay day?"

"Exactly," Jim confirmed. "Why make it easier for the capitalists to make more profit by shoving up prices at the weekend?"

"My father used to be paid on Thursday," I said slowly. "It used to be that Wednesday was the worst day, now it's Wednesday and Thursday. Only Ger and me are working, bar the post stuff, and you know the pay there."

Jim nodded. "So, Thursday will be pay day here. You know that there'll be a bit of a bonus at Christmas for you? It's service-related so it'll be small. I'll check with the finance people and we might anticipate it, pay it in advance, to give you a chance to catch up on your Christmas shopping and that. All right?"

I went out with tears in my eyes, and when I told my mother later what Jim had said and gave her the bottle from the chemist's, she had to blink fiercely to keep the tears back.

"Sometimes it's very good to know there's good people in the world. The problem is you meet them so seldom," she said slowly. "Maybe there's a lesson there for all of us."

CHAPTER FIFTEEN

I NOW WALKED most of the way in to work from Donnybrook each day to save a few bob, so I'd ample time to think about things.

It was bad at home, there was no doubt about that. There was no way at all that further cuts could be made in how we lived. We were down to the bare bone. That was the physical bit, and in a way it was easier to deal with than the emotional bit. My father was normally an easygoing man, but working for as long as he had in private service had made him soft, not streetwise, so he found it difficult to cope with his new situation.

He was angry and he couldn't vent that anger, not on us, not on my mother, and not on the petty bureaucrats who now dictated how we lived, such as the Vincent de Paul man or the local parish priest, who could help us if they so wished. So he withdrew inside himself and nobody could reach him.

My mother had a health problem too. I didn't know what it was, but I'd seen Mrs Jennings and herself in earnest secret conversation. The bit I'd overheard was Mrs Jennings saying to my mother, "Peg, sooner or later you'll have to have it done. You just can't go on as you are." They'd stopped and talked about something totally different when they saw me there. My imagination ran riot about what that might be.

In work, too, things were tough. We'd to do the ordinary nitty-gritty work and also write the new registers and shop stewards' books, and get all outstanding money in, while paying out commission to almost all the collectors. Our own internal accounting system was on a countdown to a specific date at the end of the year, a target that had to be met.

And, of course, there were the members now unemployed from the companies where the owners had legged it. They had to be met sympathetically, their claims dealt with, and possibilities of re-employment explored. That was the first time I dealt with a collective group of workers.

"Look, would you do something for me?" Jim asked me. "I've to go out to meet the social welfare people, and Sadie is down in Balbriggan. Would you meet that group of members from Dolan's? You know, the place where the workers were left high and dry? They'll be in about eleven this morning. Put them into my room. All right?"

"Ask them to wait?"

"No, no. I don't know how long I'll be, and some of them will have children with them. No. See if you can get some information from them. Let's see, what do I need? Names and addresses. Social welfare numbers, if they have them, and tax numbers. Ask them their age and marital status; be careful with those. Find out what they earned last week and if there is any money outstanding: back wages, holiday money, stuff like that. Can you do it?"

"I. . . I suppose so."

"Good girl. They have to face enough bureaucracy as it is. This will make it easier for them. For many of them we're the only hope they have left to cling to. I wouldn't want them to have to go away and come back later. You understand?"

I nodded, butterflies doing a bit of a clog dance in the pit of my stomach.

When the members came in they were all women. I asked them to go into Jim's office, and they filled it almost to overflowing. The babel of voices raised to a crescendo each time somebody new arrived.

At 11.15 I took a notebook and a couple of pens in my hands, took a deep breath, knocked on the door and went in as quickly as I could, doing my best to keep a smile on my face. The group parted to make way for me, and I noted that every chair in the place was occupied, some with two perched awkwardly on the same chair; a few kids milled around on the floor.

"Sorry for the crush," I said quickly. "The big hall is absolutely freezing at this time of day, and we'd be rattling around like peas in a very large pod. So, I think we're better off here squashed than down there freezing, don't you agree?"

There was a bit of a laugh and a few said, "Ah, sure, it's OK. Don't worry about that."

I decided to press on quickly. "Jim Gilhooley, your branch secretary, had hoped to meet you this morning. But at the last minute he got an appointment in the Department of Social Welfare with senior civil servants to talk about the problems you're facing. He's been trying really hard for the last two days to get that meeting, and, of course, it was too good an opportunity to miss. So he asked me to apologise to you on his behalf."

I paused for a moment to get my breath and to assess the reaction. "I'm May O'Brien," I said. "I work for Jim here in the office. I'm a clerical worker, not long left school. This is the first time I've ever done anything like this, and I must say I find it a bit scary."

There was a distinct easing of tension in the atmosphere. A bit of smiling, a sitting back in the chairs. One woman slipped off a shoe to ease her aching bunion. I took out a couple of pages from the copybook and brandished them.

"So I wonder would you help me? Jim said he wanted some

information that'd help him with the case he's making for you. I've written out the sort of stuff he wants on these pages. Maybe between yourselves you could sort out the info he needs. You see, I've to man the phone outside. If I don't, anyone ringing might think the union's done a runner!"

As if on cue the phone rang outside and I paused, unsure what to do next. A big, buxom, motherly woman held her hand out for the pages.

"You get on with your work, girl. Sure, we'll work away on the stuff that's needed. Me and Margie will write everything down. That will mean whoever is finished first can go. There's no need to hang around when the information is down in black and white. Isn't that so, girls?"

The two scribes were the last to leave, and when I tried to thank them they wouldn't have it.

"We were glad to do it. There you are, eighteen names and addresses, ages. Those who are serving their time—twenties, thirties, forties, fifties—that kind of thing. Marital state, now 'M' is married, 'W' is widowed, 'S' is single, and 'P' is a parent, married or single. Everything you asked is there. Everybody is due holiday money and a back week, but only the long-service people have tax or social welfare numbers. The rest never saw anything official at all; that bastard was taking the money off them just the same. It's all there."

When Jim was looking through his post, I put the pages of the copybook in front of him.

"That's the Dolan meeting information you asked for. The two women, Carmel and Margie, were real nice. They did it all, no bother."

He scanned through the sheets quickly. "What was the first thing you said," he asked, looking at me a bit quizzically. I thought for a moment.

"M'm. I apologised to them. They were crushed in here, but I said the big room would be freezing, and it was better maybe to be squashed than frozen—something like that. I told them I was a new girl, only working here a few weeks, and I was a bit scared of meeting them. Was that wrong?"

Jim laughed. "Just about perfect, I'd say. How did you get them to do the job for you?"

"I asked them. I said I had to answer the phone or people ringing up might think we'd done a runner too."

"Exactly. You handled it very well. Most times our members want to do things for themselves. We can't assume nobody can do the job like us. All they want very often is just to be given the go-ahead and to know we're all on the one tack. How did you feel yourself?"

"I was scared at first, not knowing if I could find the right words, but then, well, quite pleased with myself."

"Good girl. It was unfair to throw the thing at you, but I'd no option. I got to meet the secretary of the department to talk about this business of employers legging it and leaving the workers bereft, their social welfare stamps not even paid."

That night at home Ger whispered while I was drying up after the tea, "Meet me and Con when you're finished at Keating's corner. OK?"

I was astonished. "But. . ."

"I can't talk now. We'll see you there."

Eileen wanted to come with me, but I fobbed her off and then trotted down to Keating's corner where Ger was already waiting.

"Why. . ."

"Hold on. Con's coming." We could indeed hear Con whistling and rattling a stick along the public park rails.

"So what's up?" Con said, hunkering down on the pavement to get out of the wind.

"We've got to talk about Christmas. Neither the ma nor the da can, and Santa's got to do his usual trip down the chimney for the kids."

We hunkered down beside Con. "So what can we do?" I asked.

"Well, I've put a few bob down on that book, the Black Bob thing," Ger said. "It'll only need a clean-up. There's smoke damage, not much, but a good rubber and patience. . ."

"I'll do it," I said. "We'll need to get it now in case somebody else goes for it." I reached for my purse. "How much d'ye need?"

"Another half a crown. Could I leave it in to you at Liberty Hall? You couldn't do it at home."

"I'll do it in my lunch hour. Now, there's the doll for Kate. It's bought and the clothes will be ready in time, but if we could get a cot or something to put it in, it'd look so much better."

Ger looked at Con. "How big is the doll?" Con asked. I measured her size with my hands.

Con nodded. "Can do," he said laconically. "Just a box really, but it'd be nice if we could line it and put a pillow in it."

"There's the bits bag," I said slowly. All the "good" pieces of material were thrown into a bag to be used as patches or let downs whenever needed. "I could take a look for something suitable."

I was no seamstress and it was a daunting task. Then I had a brainwave. Eileen was a first-class sewer, and she was pining for something to do that'd take her mind off her ma.

"Yeah, Eileen will help, and we could do that, and it would make the doll look so much better than sitting on a chair or something on Christmas morning."

"Right." Ger took charge of the meeting again. "How'll you manage with the cot, Con?"

"I'll do it round in Jackie's," Con said. "It'll just be a cut-down box. I have just the thing in mind, I think, but I'll have to nick the paint out of the shed, Ger, so I'll need a bit of a diversion. This time I don't want to have to get up in the night to see if the bloody paint is dry!"

"Then there's the few gew-gaws to fill the two stockings," Ger went on unheedingly. "You know, a few sweets, an orange, a banana, a bar of chocolate, a few new pennies in a bit of tinsel, a few little bits and pieces I can get down in Moore Street and Henry Street when things get cheaper."

"And the ma and da?" I asked. "I don't know. . ." There was silence for a moment.

"Cigarettes for the da," Con said. "It's all we can do. It'll be easier for him after Christmas Eve when the post is over. He'll be able to sit back, and a few cigarettes will help. We can leave them till nearer the time, Ger, isn't that right?"

Ger nodded and looked at me. "And the ma?"

"Maybe we can get gloves or a warm scarf. She feels the cold so much. That's all I can think of anyway," I said. "I'll look around the shops at lunchtime and see if there's anything she'd like."

"And us?" Con asked with a smile on his face.

"The hand of friendship, the warmth of a good fire and the smile of the infant Jesus," we said together, laughing as we got to our feet and stamped around to get our circulation moving again. That was a quote from Con's spiritual director, who believed we'd succumbed to all the evils of the commer cialisation of Christmas. It'd become something of a family joke, since the man himself enjoyed nothing more than a generous portion of hot punch and bore all its marks.

CHAPTER SIXTEEN

JIM HAD DECIDED to send out circulars to all our shop stewards before Christmas. This was my first big challenge in the circulars department.

There were three separate sheets. The first gave our opening hours over the Christmas period, with a plea to have all outstanding monics in before the year's end. The second conveyed seasonal greetings from the general officers and staff of the union to all branch members. And the third was a sort of "state of the union" info pack. It named recently recruited employments, the three that had closed down and the numbers of members who'd be out of work as a result, and a brief outline of the legal situation where social welfare stamps were deducted but not paid by employers, and the legal entitlements for the bank holidays and so on.

I slaved over the stencils, trying to make sure they were perfect. Then I went down to Frances to roll them off on the Gestetner. She was engaged in some sort of crisis, so I did the usual check that my teacher advised to ensure that the ink and paper were OK and started rolling. Everything was going fine. Suddenly chaos loomed.

Paper spewed out, half inked, creased, pleated and torn. Hastily I switched off the machine and caught my breath. The machine was virtually inaccessible, the light was bad, and people continually brushed past. "Having trouble? That machine's a bastard!" they'd say and walk on by.

Eventually Frances appeared by my side. "I warned you," she said. She threw an expert look over the machine, re-inked it, and reset the paper. "Stand back," she said and threw the On switch, at the same time giving the machine an unmerciful belt with a chair leg that she kept handy on the floor.

"Take that, you bastard," she said, poised to give it another belt, and the machine belched a few times and then settled into doing the job it should do. She watched with satisfaction as it dutifully slid out page after page of beautifully printed script. "You have to show it who's boss," she said with a grin. "Mind you, hit it just there. That's its tender spot."

She went back to her work, and I collected the sheets into two boxes and made my way back to Eden Quay and my own office. I hadn't realised how strong the gale coming up the Liffey was until I was in the street and struggling to keep my feet and a tight grip on my two slippery boxes under my arms.

It was funny in a way, a bit like being on the deck of a ship in a gale. My progress at best was crab-like. The gale seemed determined to scatter my sheets to the four winds, and I had to keep taking refuge in doorways to get a tighter grip on them.

A man caught up with me.

"Here, let me give you a hand with those," he said and took one of the boxes from me. He was one of the men from the shop. "Jackie Mooney's my name. I've seen you in the shop."

We started off again, a sort of cartoonish four steps forward, two steps back kind of dance, his hand on my arm to steady me, and laughing when we had the breath because it was very funny. At last we reached the brown doorway, and it was very silent inside out of the wind. I took back my box and thanked him for his help.

"I'd take it upstairs for you if I'd time," he said, "but I'm due out. . ." He checked his pocket watch.

"You work. . .?" I couldn't keep my incredulity from my voice. "I mean. . . you're always in the shop. . ."

"I'm a busman," he said with a smile. "My bus is due out in fifteen minutes, and it'd never do for me to be late. I can't keep the passengers waiting."

He turned to leave. "It's kind of our little club, the shop. You see, we can't go into the pub, and you get sick of the branch room, so our group meet in the shop. Sure, it's home from home since it's ITGWU and so are we." With that he was gone, and I trudged up the stairs with my two boxes.

As I sorted and folded the circulars and stuck them in their envelopes, I tried to work that one out. When I thought it through it made sense. It was obvious that the hotel had occupied the whole corner of Eden Quay and Beresford Place, and the union must have bought it en bloc. A union running a news agency and a pub, sure that really did seem strange.

The job done and the stamped envelopes in a box to be brought down to the post box at the front door, now I'd have time to relax.

I was on my own but felt quite capable of handling just about any situation that might arise. I didn't have to work late as Eddie the chair, Bee McCluskey and Joe Reynolds were coming in to help Jim tonight. I decided to get more coal. I slipped off my jacket, rolled up my sleeves and got the bucket, shovel and the key. I unlocked the door, shoved it back with one hand, holding the bucket and shovel in the other.

As the door groaned open a disembodied face loomed before me, spotlit by some kind of weird wavering light. The bucket and shovel fell from my hand as the face, mouth and eyes contorted, moving towards me. There was a rumble behind that leering face and then the light went out! I made no sound, bar the clanking of the bucket and shovel as they fell and rolled. I swear I lifted a foot at least off the ground and that my hair stood straight up on end. My eyes and mouth were wide open, but I was helpless. I couldn't move a muscle of my own volition. I fell on my hands and knees, and somehow the face was still there and the rumble had become more intense.

A form materialised and spoke and I realised it was Terry, but I still couldn't speak. For a few minutes we went through a kind of macabre dance as he tried to lift me and couldn't and I couldn't help in getting myself to my feet.

Eventually I found myself back in the office, a cup of tea a mouse could easily dance on in my hand, and Terry apologising profusely. I found then too that every time he'd touched me, he'd left a black palm print, so that I looked as if I'd tangled with a grizzly bear at least.

"But, Terry. . ." I said when at last I got my voice back. "Terry, why on earth. . .?"

He had the grace to look at least a bit ashamed.

"Well, it seemed a good idea at the time. You see, Mick Dunbar is at me and at me to do something for him. What he's asking is so stupid, but the man won't listen. . ."

"Terry. . ."

"Well, they're rewiring the front bit of the hall, not before it's time. . . Anyway, my hidey-holes got scarce, and I thought of the coal shed. I knew you'd got your coal in for the day. I never thought you'd be getting more."

"It's a late night, Terry. Jim will be here."

"Well, I'll be. Anyway, I'd got meself a plank on a couple of nails beat into the wall to sit on over the coal, a candle in a tin can hung on a nail and all the papers from the shop to go through. Sure, I was in me alley. . . And then you came in. I tried to speak, to tell you it was only me, but me plank gave way, the coal cascaded down and me with it, and me candle went AWOL. There you were, your hair standing straight up and your mouth wide open but not a sound to be heard."

Terry got out his pipe and began to fill it. "D'ye know what? You looked just like a ghost. You know, like the spectre from the haunted house. All it needed was clanking chains and creaking doors."

"Jesus! Terry, you're really the pits. How do you know I'm not going to have a nervous breakdown, or a heart attack? D'ye not know the damage you've done?" I looked down. "God, will you look at the cut of me? Jim and Eddie the chair and all will be in soon. What can I do?"

"Wash your face first," Terry said, standing in the doorway, "and your hands. Put on your jacket as soon as you can. If you want I'll stand by the phone till you get back."

From then on my fires were mysteriously stoked in my absence so that my journeys to the coal shed became fewer. Also, our papers and our post were delivered personally by Terry every morning first thing.

But, for me, it was quite a time before I could get out of my head that lunging white face in the black darkness of the coal shed and the accelerating rumble as the wavery light disappeared somewhere in the darkness.

CHAPTER SEVENTEEN

IT WAS ROUTINE now for me to call into the shop in the morning for the milk and whatever was needed, and to note the transaction in my little book. So this morning I swung into the doorway as usual, my mind more on money than milk. I was now three weeks over my month's probation and nothing had changed. My wages were still thirty shillings a week, and now, just two weeks before Christmas, there was still no sign of my Christmas bonus.

As the door swung behind me I stood transfixed.

Rosie, the mildest of little women, had come from behind the counter to confront a big brawny man. Both of them were so angry that they'd forgotten, or didn't care, about onlookers. It was a kind of David and Goliath confrontation. Rosie advancing, this tiny woman, eyes like rapiers, red spots of anger on her cheeks, even her gold-rimmed glasses seeming to glisten with anger, her forefinger held out like a pistol jammed into the man's midriff. He backed into a corner unable, as a man, to put a finger on this little bantam cock of a woman.

"Just say that again," she begged him, the top of her head level with his ITGWU badge, her finger poking painfully in his midriff. "Just say again what you just said about 1916. About the men and the women of the Irish Citizen Army. Just mention again Connolly, a man who died to let scum like you live, you slimy, slithery toad! Say that again about 1916 and I'll see you crawl back under the stone you crawled out from under. You know nothing, believe in nothing and have respect for nothing. You don't deserve to have standing space on this planet."

Nellie pulled at her arm. "Rosie. Oh God, Rosie. Don't get yourself upset. He's not worth it. Oh Rosie, please. . .There's the customers. . .Oh Rosie, please. . ."

Rosie threw off Nellie's hand. "Don't interfere, Nellie. It's not your fight."

She drew herself up to her full four foot, eleven inches height and faced the man again.

"You've insulted my comrades," she spat at him. "You've danced on dead men's graves. You've insulted the men and women who defied an empire to obtain freedom. Who paid in blood, again and again, and for what? For scum like you? For freedom for men who don't even know the meaning of the word!"

"I only said. . ." the man said, trying to move back into the ranks of the other men who, markedly, weren't supporting him.

"Was what we went through worth it?" Rosie asked herself as much as anyone else there, drawing back from him. "Was the pain and the anguish and the blood that was shed, all the sacrifices, was it for nothing after all?" She looked up at him, her eyes tear-filled. "Jesus Christ, did they die for nothing?"

There was silence for a moment.

"I only meant. . ." The man was hushed by his colleagues and bundled out of the shop. Nellie took Rosie's arm and led her to the back of the shop, trying to comfort her. Jackie Mooney took over shop assistant duties and handed me the milk.

"That was awful. . ." he started and began busily tidying things away.

"Yes," I nodded. "What started it?"

"He's more mouth than brain," Jackie said. "Tries to do the big fellow and always ends up looking like a halfwit. He said we should never have been neutral in the war, should have gone in with Britain as our natural ally, and then we'd have more jobs and more money. Naturally enough Rosie saw it as an insult to those who fought for our freedom from Britain, and who died for it. Then one word borrowed another. God, I hate that kind of argument."

Back in the office Terry had left the post on the counter. I quickly scanned the letters and saw one that seemed as though it might be the one from head office I was waiting for. I placed it on top of the pile on Jim's desk so that he'd open it first.

I was settled down typing a rough draft of an agreement that Jim had given me to do when Golly poked his head around the door.

"Tea's up," he said, quietly for him, but I'm sure it still could be heard around in Abbey Street. "Whenever you're ready."

I felt a bit of a sinking-heart feeling. I'd have to go. There was no doubt about that. I'd done some typing work for Tommy, and he'd invited me for tea one morning this week.

Golly opened the door with a flourish. My hand was enveloped in his bear's paw, he welcomed me in, and I was deposited in a chair at the desk. I was hit by the tidal wave of heat and could feel myself wilting.

"No cream cakes," Tommy said. "Sorry about that. The budget wouldn't allow it. We're on the clippings of tin at the moment. Isn't that right, Paddy?"

Paddy McLoughlin nodded and winked from his desk where he was interviewing a man about something.

"That's right, Tommy. You invited the lady to Pauperville. We can't even treat her decent."

"True. True for you, Paddy. Them bastards in Finance. I bet

they have cream cakes every day. Chocolate éclairs. God, I'd give my right arm for one of them right now."

I knew from the correspondence that Tommy was in trouble about his cash returns and other routine matters. Jim Gilhooley did his every Monday and was scrupulous about receipts and balances and responding to correspondence. Tommy was not, by nature, the most methodical of men and worked on the basis, more in hope than certainty, that his returns would achieve some sort of balance.

Golly was on one knee at the fire, which was, as usual, hotter than any other fire I've ever seen. The black-encrusted billycan was seething away on the hob, and he shook in tea leaves from cone-shaped newspaper twists, so that the leaves danced on top of the water like dervishes. Into the seething cauldron he tossed a matchstick. Catching my eye on him, he said with a grin, "Stops the tea getting smoked."

Tommy smoothed a newspaper over his desk, carelessly consigning bundles of correspondence to no-man's land behind his desk in the process. He took out a loaf of bread, took a knife from Golly's belt holster and started cutting thick wedges of bread and spreading them with butter.

Golly placed five mugs on the desk and a couple of twisted and bent spoons. I looked at the mugs with respect and some trepidation. Each was thick, probably unbreakable and about the size of a one-pound jam jar.

A lemonade bottle of milk was lifted out of a haversack and a twist of sugar uncovered. Tommy used the corkscrew on Golly's knife to puncture the tin of condensed milk. Golly was over at the wall inspecting the shovels. He took one down and ran his hand across the blade. Then, to my surprise, he brought it over to the fire and manoeuvred it so that the blade rested over the fire, the handle on the rungs of a chair.

He took a pile of newspapers down to the hearthstone and knelt down beside it. Quite casually he broke three eggs on to the shovel blade and manoeuvred them with his knife and a bent twisted fork so that they were frying evenly. When they were done on one side, with a dextrous flick of the shovel he turned the eggs until that side was done too. Then he slid them on to a platter warming on the hearthstone. The eggs were then replaced by rashers and sausages and a half ring each of black and white pudding. When all was cooked, he brought the platter to the desk and went back for the billycan. To my amazement, he took it up by the wire handle, his hand protected by his neck cloth, and giving himself room, swung the billycan over his head.

He looked a bit like the altar boy who swings the thurible with the incense at Benediction. He caught my eye and saw my mystification. "That's to draw the tea," he grinned.

That done, he poured the tea into the mugs, slapped a fried egg, a sausage split in two, and a rasher between two slices of bread, and handed it to me. "That'll keep you going till dinner time," he grinned. "Put hair on your. . . Oh God! Better not finish that."

"That's a building site brekkie," Paddy said and grinned. "It'll put a bit of flesh on your bones."

The tea was almost solid in the mug. I think you could actually have sliced it if you were so inclined, but the sandwich was delicious.

When I got back, I kept my eye open for Jim, for his reaction to his correspondence. He called me into his office after a few minutes. I brought in the work I'd completed, and we worked out the responses that'd be made on various issues. Then he took up the letter from head office.

"This is what we've both been waiting on," he said with some satisfaction. He straightened out the letter and began to doodle on a spare piece of paper. "You're confirmed as a permanent member of the clerical staff of the union. Your wages have gone up to three pounds ten shillings. Now, as I already said, there will be deductions from that."

He jotted down some figures on the paper. "Let's see. Social welfare, tax, pension, union deductions—what else?" He totted up his figures and rechecked them. "You'll have three pounds and fourpence each week to take home. That's back-dated to the date your probation ended." He checked his figures again. "So the difference is one pound ten shillings and fourpence multiplied by three. Then you have also got your Christmas bonus. That's four pounds. Not bad really with your short service. So the grand total is. . . eight pounds eleven shillings. Isn't that right?" He turned his tot around to me to check it. It was right. I could hardly talk.

He opened his cash box and counted out the money and stuck it into an envelope, marking on the envelope the amount enclosed. He shook my hand and wished me a long and happy working relationship within the union.

Then I found myself back at my desk, the envelope in my purse and the purse jammed down into my coat pocket for security. The money would make such a hugh difference!

I was meeting Ger at lunchtime. We had the book for Kevin. It was now as clean as a new whistle. We had the doll for Kate, though the clothes were not yet finished. Eileen was still working on the cot pillow and bedspread. Con had the cot made, and it had only to be painted. The stocking fillers still had to be got. Well, now we could be generous. We could throw in a few fun things just for the kick of seeing the wonder on the kids' faces on Christmas morning. We could get the scarf for my mother and the cigarettes for my father. We could do much better now that the money was safe in my pocket.

I resolved to get together with my mother, Ger and Con to get the best food we could to make this Christmas as enjoyable as we possibly could. Maybe even a Christmas tree. . .?

CHAPTER EIGHTEEN

THAT WAS A good lunch break. The money in my purse made a difference, of course. We had a sit-down meal of egg and chips, followed by fruit sundaes, and we talked. It was the first time Ger and I were out together as adults. That's so different from the bickering and rivalries of childhood that, at first, things were a bit stilted. But as we settled down in the atmosphere of warmth, conviviality and pre-Christmas cheer, with hot food inside us, gradually the barriers came down.

Ger admitted to being depressed about his situation. He wanted a decent job, he wanted more money, more security, and he wanted, more than anything, to get married before he became middle-aged. The choices he had, as he saw them, were limited. He was now too tall to go as a bus driver or conductor. He might get into the railway as a fireman on the steam engines. He reckoned he had the strength and commitment to do the physically hard job involved. The money was good, but the hours were atrocious. He had a pal on the beet run, and it was an around-the-clock workload in season to get the beet to the sugar factories as fast as possible. His friend, with his mates, had slept in a wagon on the tracks for the sugar beet season.

"The problem," Ger said, "is that the deliveries by rail had to be made with the least possible disruption of the ordinary rail schedule. So they do a lot of late night or early morning runs, but the money he said he'd made. Well. . ."

We thought about that for a moment in silence.

"The alternative," Ger went on, "is for me to go to England or somewhere. Work on the building sites. All the building that's going on over there. . ." But he evidently didn't want to go away, and who could blame him?

"And you?" Ger asked.

I thought for a moment. "I'd be perfectly happy to stay where I am. If I can, that is. It's more than a job. There's something worthwhile about it."

"Changing the world?" he laughed as we got up to go.

I smiled too as we buttoned up coats and pulled up coat collars to face the arctic wind outside, but I felt deep inside that what he'd said was perfectly true. The trade union movement was trying to change the world.

It was trying to make it possible for him to achieve the perfectly natural desire to marry and have a family while he was still a comparatively young man. But most of all, not to always fear, as we did, what might happen tomorrow to grind that ambition into the dust.

We hurried down to Henry Street where the street traders demonstrated all the Christmas stocking fillers to eager and enthusiastic customers. There were monkeys that danced, ballet dancers that twirled, jack-in-the-boxes that popped, acrobats that swung and cars that looped the loop against all the principles of gravity.

We watched and laughed, suddenly kids again, pointing out wonders to each other. Christmas carols were sung by choirs at street corners, and the buskers vied with them. Coloured balloons danced in the wind, and Santa Claus lived on almost every stand. Holly wreaths, mistletoe, tinsel ornaments, Christmas cheer were all around us. In Moore Street the traders sang out their wares all at the top of their voices and with an odd few scathing witticisms thrown in for good measure.

We felt we were on an expeditionary mission, checking over what we could get for stocking fillers. In a doorway we conferred, me holding tightly on to my purse squashed into my coat pocket. "What do you think, Ger?"

"The lead set of cowboys and Indians for Kevin," Ger answered quickly. "He could play for hours with them, particularly the ones with the Indian chief on the pinto pony. He does look imposing."

"It's a bit dear," I hesitated. "I mean. . ."

He looked at me sideways. "It's bloody well Christmas," he said flatly, kicking at a stone on the ground. "Can't he have some fun at four years of age?"

I nodded slowly "He'll never be four again. Right. And Kate. Either that little delph teaset. . .Did you see the cute little teapot? Or the pencil box with the blue flowers on it. I can't choose. . ."

"The teaset." Ger was decisive. "You bring a pencil box to school and it becomes a school thing, but the teaset will be at home when she comes in. She'll treasure it all the more as her own thing."

"OK. That's settled so. I'm holding out new pennies from the union cash. I told Jim what I was doing, and it's OK as long as the balance is right. So maybe six new shiny pennies each for Kate and Kevin wrapped up in tinsel paper, and a rosy apple and an orange each. A bar of Cadbury's chocolate each, plain for Kate and nutty for Kevin. And. . ."

"Hang on there. The kitty's got a bottom to it don't forget. We've to think of the ma and da too."

"And Con. God, he's still only thirteen. Could we. . .?"

Ger kicked the inoffensive stone again, eyes intently on it as he thought. "He'd love a knife," he said quietly. "You know, with all the gadgets, but we can't spend all your money. I've little or none, nor any expectations either. You need some things for yourself. I mean, I know about your shoes, the hole's got really bad now, and this weather. I know you're doing without your lunch."

I punched his arm. "Ger, we're looking at Christmas presents here. Now where's your Christmas spirit? Will you price the knife and we'll talk about it later? Maybe we could swing it, why not? And I've been thinking about the da. Maybe a pair of carpet slippers would be good to ease his feet after all the walking. He has never had slippers. I could get a pair, not too gaudy, in Clery's for less than ten shillings. And a blouse for the ma, a lovely pale blue, for just a bit more. What d'ye think?"

"Sounds good." Ger wasn't quite meeting my eye. I shook his arm.

"Ger, I want us all to have as good a Christmas as we can, and I know you do too. So what's wrong?"

He pulled his coat collar tighter as heavy sleety rain cleared the street of people. "I have to go."

"Ger. . ."

"Well. A man should be able to contribute something decent to the kitty. All I have is my wages and the few bob I get for sorting the periodicals. I'll get a few tips at Christmas, but that's it. There's no way I can get more money as I am, no matter how hard I work, no matter how hard I try. I get disheartened."

I touched his sleeve. "I know, Ger. It's the system that's wrong. It shouldn't be like this. You're right. We'll both have to go back to work now. We'll leave the stocking fillers until nearer the big day when they'll be cheaper, and easier to hide. But you know the kind of thing we've in mind. Will you look after that, Ger?"

We started to walk back down the street with the rain still

pelting down, he to go to Batchelor's Walk, me to Liberty Hall. Ger agreed, suggesting that if he saw the set of cowboys and Indians or the teaset getting scarce on the stalls, he should buy immediately to save us being disappointed. I agreed and hand-ed over enough cash to cover that possibility.

We stopped at the corner of Abbey Street. "Ger," I said, "I sug-gest we get the ma aside tonight and tell her what we plan. Not about her present, nor Con's, but our ideas. And we can talk about Christmas food—see what we can manage there too. I know she's worried about that. OK?"

We parted, he waiting until I got across the road safely in the Christmas traffic, and I smiled a bit to myself, absurdly touched at the gesture of the elder brother.

When I got to the office, Jim noted my drenched coat and took it off the coat stand to hang it close to the fire to dry. "Shops packed?" he commiserated.

"Yes. Today, me and Ger were out on a pricing expedition. We'll buy nearer to Christmas. It was fun though, despite the rain."

"Maybe you'd want to get home a bit early tonight," Jim said, engrossed in the work he was doing on the register. "Not to work late, I mean. Now you've got your back money."

I looked at him in surprise. "Oh no. The work has to be done and there's so little time left. No, I'll do my stint tonight, no bother."

At around six o'clock I replenished the coal buckets, filled the kettle and set out the tea things. Sadie was down with Peg O'Donnell in the Hotel Branch but would be back.

Eddie the chair, Bee McCluskey and Joe Sheridan were due in from work to join us, so I set their places too. Jim excused himself, saying he'd pick up the evening paper in the shop before his tea.

Paddy McLoughlin put his head in the door as soon as the tea was made. "Is my name in the pot?" he asked with great good humour. I put out another cup and more biscuits and hoped there'd be enough milk for what now was heading towards a tea party.

Eddie the chair and Bee came in together. Both worked in Polikoff's, he as a cutter, and she as a presser. Women tended not to be pressers in the men's trade, so Bee was an exceptional woman. Eddie was a dark, dapper little man, always impeccably turned out. Unfortunately he saw himself as quite a ladies' man and worked assiduously at the role, but with little success as far as I could see. Now he came in, grinning from ear to ear, arms outstretched to hug me, and I automatically stepped out of his reach. "Well, how is my favourite little cutie?" he declaimed theatrically.

"Gene Kelly," I said. "God, can you never get anything that's original?"

He leered, doing a Groucho Marx imitation, and I started to pour the tea. Jim came in with a box of cakes from the Kylemore Bakery, and Bee piled them up on a plate in the centre of the desk. "Good Lord!" Joe Sheridan exclaimed. "Jim, you're living dangerously. Ye'll never get rid of us now!"

It was a convivial little gathering. Bee was, I suppose, in her forties but always dressed in the latest of fashions, wore the latest make-up and jewellery, her hair coiffed in the then-current hairdo. You'd never think looking at her that she earned her living standing in the steam over a Hoffman press as she pressed the line of garments that always stood waiting on the rack beside her. And always under pressure from her supervisor to get the stuff "OUT—OUT". She was from Mayo and had a dry sense of humour and was always capable of taking Eddie down to size.

Joe, on the contrary, was a man with a distinct English accent, though he too came from the West. He'd been active in the IRA in the bomb campaign during the war years in Britain and had something of a past. Because of his accent, he tended to be taken for an outsider in Irish union circles but was actually a committed trade unionist.

For his trade union activities he was not on good terms with his employer, a hosiery manufacturer in Patrick Street, and was apparently destined always to end up on the night shift of the knitters in the company.

Since he wouldn't be allowed to collect the union contributions on the premises, he was forced to stand outside the gate to make the collection as the workers went into work or came out. That meant he stayed on after his night shift ended to collect the money and came back in after a few hours sleep to get the rest on their way out at five o'clock. He did that month after month with not the slightest complaint about the hardship involved. He was also one of the nicest men you could meet, with his own droll sense of humour.

The cakes were doled out and eaten, topped up with a few biscuits. Bee and I cleared the stuff away, washed up and came back to find everybody deeply engrossed in their work. Eddie, Bee and Joe were used to "Music while you work", so either the radio would be switched on or, if there was only "rubbishy talk" on, they'd sing themselves as they worked. Their repertoire was varied. They could sing the latest hits or go back to the oldies that everybody could join in. A few bars of a song would be recognised immediately. "That's good, that is, it'll last," was the highest accolade they could give to a song.

As we worked, visitors called in, drawn in by the sounds of jollity: Terry, Frank Robbins, Paddy, Tommy and Golly from next door, and Tom O'Reilly from the Food Branch. Seeing Tom made me wonder again how on earth he'd got the name "Two-Gun" O'Reilly. I asked Jim and he laughed.

"Oh, you thought he was a gunman. Tom O'Reilly! Far from it. No, it's not that. You see, Tom is missing every Thursday from the branch. It's his time off. You know how it is, night meetings and all that. You're entitled to take time off to compensate. So Tom's out of the branch on a Thursday afternoon, and you'd be forgiven for thinking he was sitting at home in Clontarf with a whiskey and soda at his elbow and drawing on a Winston Churchill-sized cigar. The truth is far different. Everybody knows that if you need Tom on a Thursday afternoon, you go up to the Corinthian cinema and ask the usherette to get him from the parterre. The other name for the Corinthian cinema is 'the ranch' because it shows only cowboy films. Tom goes to them all. He's an expert on the bang-bang film industry. So he's called 'Two-Gun' O'Reilly."

I was really surprised. What Jim said didn't at all fit with my own impression of Tom O'Reilly. I remembered the watchful, pale blue, expressionless eyes so at variance with his hail-fellow-well-met outward appearance. He was a fan of the bang-bang films? It didn't add up.

"Is it true, Jim, that 'Two-Gun' sailed his yacht over to the Liffey wall from Clontarf one morning to avoid the morning traffic rush?" Eddie asked with a grin. "Did he climb up the iron ladder on the quay wall and saunter over to the Hall in his whites and with a skipper's cap on his head?"

"So the story goes," Jim said with a smile. He looked at his watch. "Time we packed it up," he said. "It's nearly nine o'clock. I've the car. I can leave either the southsiders or the northsiders home. Which will it be?"

Joe had his "chug-chug" Honda with him, and he offered Eddie a lift on the back. There were much ribald pleasantries as they set off for the north side of the city. Jim took Bee and myself home on the south side, he himself then going on to Kimmage to his own home.

When I turned the key in the hall door, my mother came through from the kitchen. "Want something to eat?" she asked. "You're working very long hours. I'm a bit worried about you."

"No need," I said. "I'm fine. And I got my back money. And I'm permanent in the job!"

"Good for you." She squeezed my shoulder as we went through to the kitchen. "That's really good news."

I put the kettle on to make a cup of tea and we sat at the table together.

"Ger said you wanted a bit of a talk with me," she said. "Your father's on his last round of the day. Honest to God, his postbag gets heavier and heavier each day. Besides the blisters on his feet, he's got a patch of skin missing on his hip the size of the palm of your hand where the bag rubbed the skin away like a bit of sandpaper."

Ger and Con came in, reporting that Kate and Kevin were safely tucked away in bed. Silently I added another two cups to the table and sat down to wait for the kettle to boil.

"I got my back money and I'm permanent," I said proudly. "Jim got the letter today. Look." I upended the purse and the money cascaded out on to the table. "We're rich!"

My mother sat, elbows on the table, hands covering her mouth and looked at it. "Fair play to you," she said slowly. "You've done well."

"It's ours," I said. "My take-home pay from now on will be three pounds and fourpence, every week, imagine that! It'll make things easier. Me and Ger had a talk today about Santa Claus and all that stuff. You know? Making sure good old Santa Claus comes down the chimney on the day for Kate and Kevin."

I explained about the doll's cot that would, in time, be paint-ed, and have a pillow and bedspread.

"The cot will be pink, with roses on it," Con said proudly. "It'll look nice. I promise you that."

I told them about the teaset with the cute little teapot, the Black Bob book, which now looked as good as new and the box of lead cowboys and Indians with the war chief on the pinto pony, and how we would get the stocking fillers nearer to Christ-mas when the prices went down a bit.

My mother was totally surprised. "But how can you. . ."

"We want your advice," I said quickly. "For Da we thought we would get a pair of carpet slippers, to ease his feet, and a few cig-arettes for when he can sit back and take it easy. What d'ye think?"

She sipped her tea and slowly put the cup back down in the saucer. "That's a great idea, but you need shoes and a new coat. You can't. . ."

"It's our Christmas too," Ger said quietly, "and the kids will only be four and five once in their lives."

"We have to do the best we can," said Con, sitting up straighter, "to make Christmas count. If we don't we lose every-thing, even hope. I know Da's going through a hard time, but when the Christmas post is over, please God there'll be some-thing better. If we let go Christmas, we'll all sink together. That's what I think."

My mother patted his arm. "Good lad," she said slowly. "Now, your father'll be coming in soon, and I want to have his meal ready for him, so what can I do?"

"We want to talk about the Christmas dinner, about what we could have. Could we get a bit of roast beef? What d'ye think?"

"With roast potatoes," Con said, "and gravy. I suppose a trifle would be out of the question?"

"A cake with icing, with a snowman on it." Ger said with a laugh. "Do you remember how I nearly swallowed the snowman when I was four?"

My mother laughed too at the memory. "God, you put the heart across me, Ger, that Christmas," she said. "Well, you've given me a bit of heart for facing into Christmas and that's the truth. You're right, Christmas is for all of us, and particularly for the smaller ones, and we mustn't forget that. Thanks, kids." And off she went to look after my father.

CHAPTER NINETEEN

Next day when I went into the shop for the milk, Rosie was on her own behind the counter. She smiled mildly, her hand on the bottle of milk.

"Just the milk today?" she asked.

I nodded, checking my book, then waved to Frances who had stopped with someone in the shop doorway, laughing at something the man said.

Rosie looked at me sharply. "You've lost weight, May," she said accusingly. "You're not trying to be like your woman?" nodding her head at Frances. "Don't do it. Never interfere with nature, child."

I had lost weight; walking more and eating less obviously had its effect. I'd thought it an improvement, that I was getting a woman's figure, rather than that of a gawky girl.

She leaned towards me, this tiny little woman, and said, "When you've seen the effects of a hunger strike on the human body, it never goes out of your mind, child. So promise me you won't abuse your body by cutting down on eating."

"I won't," I promised. "It's just. . . well, things are a bit difficult at home. You know how it is."

"And little ones at home?"

"Two—five and four."

Rosie nodded soberly. "Did you know there's a tin of Jacob's biscuits here with your name on it? It's a Christmas gift from the shop. You can collect it the day before Christmas Eve. All right?"

I fiddled with the top of the bottle of milk, nearly knocking it to the ground in the process. Clumsily I retrieved it. Rosie waited.

"Can I ask you something?"

"Certainly, ask away."

"Yesterday. . . when you had the row with that man, did you really mean what you said? About not knowing if it was worth it. The sacrifices and all, I mean."

Rosie stood still, her arms folded across her chest. "So?"

"Well, Frank Robbins told me about the Countess, Madame, and how she was like a brilliant light with her talk about Finn MacCool and all that. My question really is, what happened to women since? Even here in Liberty Hall, where the struggle took place, women don't seem to have a voice."

Rosie stood for a moment in silence. "Madame was in Holloway Jail, you know, when she stood for that Westminster seat in the House of Commons. She was elected, though, of course, she didn't take her seat. She couldn't take the oath of allegiance to a foreign king. Every other woman candidate in Britain was wiped out in that General Election of 1918, including Christabel Pankhurst from the Suffragette movement.

"So why have women been excluded? It's because men hold the power to themselves, then, now and always. Do you know which commandant in 1916 wouldn't have women in his assigned position?"

I shook my head. "I don't know."

"De Valera. And who is in power now? De Valera. Does that answer your question?"

"But Connolly. . ."

"Connolly is dead, and with him died our dreams."

"But. . ."

"It's your fight now, girl. You and young ones like you. We've done our stint. Did Frank tell you how Madame died?"

I shook my head.

"In 1927 in Sir Patrick Dunne's Hospital in a public ward, old, tired and worn out. The Free State wouldn't allow a state funeral nor let her lie in the City Hall nor the Mansion House, so she ended up in the Rotunda because that wasn't state property.

"Her Fianna boys stood guard over her coffin, and something like 100,000 people filed by to pay their respects. There were eight lorryloads of flowers, huge bouquets and tiny little posies, and seven bands. There were representatives from Sinn Féin, the Fianna, all the women's organisations, the unions, including our own, and the Citizen Army and Fianna Fáil. But there were a hundred Free State soldiers in Glasnevin graveyard to make sure Madame didn't get a military salute over her grave. Instead her Citizen Army uniform covered her coffin as it was lowered into the ground."

"My God! But why. . .?"

"Dev gave the oration over her grave, it's true. But Madame would never have taken the oath of loyalty to the Crown! She said herself she could never face Jimmy Connolly or Paddy Pearse in the hereafter if she did."

Rosie started checking the cash in the till, and I realised our conversation was over.

"Thanks for telling me, Rosie." I said awkwardly.

"Don't forget to pick up them biscuits, child."

As I moved off I wondered how on earth such a mild-looking little woman had managed to live through such turbulent times. I concluded, as I trudged up the stairs, that she had more strength in her little finger than I had in my whole body.

CHAPTER TWENTY

ABBIE WAS COMING home! Eileen was overjoyed. She couldn't stop talking, planning and wondering about how she'd be. What would she think of the preparations they'd all made to welcome her home?

Mrs Jennings had been in to see Abbie in the hospital and had talked to nurses and doctors about what was involved.

"It's just a Christmas break," she insisted to all who'd listen. "The danger isn't over. Abbie's health has improved and the babbie isn't in acute danger. Abbie must keep off her feet or we'll be back where we started. You do all understand that?"

As a result, the daybed was transferred into a small back bedroom, and the boys who'd been sleeping there were farmed out on a temporary basis to neighbours to make room. "Your ma must rest. She mustn't be bothered with problems, and Josephine, you sleep with your mother. Every night. You understand. . .?"

Josephine nodded, knowing exactly what was involved. Eileen would continue to stay with us to make room in her own house, but her heart would be there amidst all the excitement.

Josephine and her father went in on the Sunday to collect Abbie. In their house everything was polished and shining, even the kids. The neighbours, including ourselves, kept a wary eye out for the ambulance that was to deliver her home. When we heard it, we all moved to the door to welcome her, her own children in the place of honour. Abbie looked paler, smaller, more worn than before, but she also was on the verge of tears as the ambulance men, with a bit of good-humoured joking, manoeuvred her in a sort of chair through the narrow door and into her home.

The kids were all kissed and hugged, then Mrs Jennings shooed them away while she looked after Abbie. Abbie's husband, Tony O'Dowd, looked around the house at a bit of a loss as to what to do, then folded his newspaper to the horse-racing page, with its results and forecasts for the next week's racing, and made his way by a roundabout course to join his pals in the pub when the Holy Hour was over.

My mother raised her eyes to heaven. "And Abbie thought he was pining for her?" she remarked dryly. "Will we ever learn?"

On Monday when I got to work, I was told there'd be a bit of a do in the hall in the Hotel Branch the following evening after work. The general president, vice president and general secretary would attend, and we were all expected to be present at half-six.

"For what?" I asked Paddy McLoughlin.

"For what? Well, I like that! For the honour of meeting your boss men, that's what, and to be told to 'Put your shoulder to the wheel, your nose to the grindstone,' and 'To tighten your belt' all at the same time. That's what. Of course, you'll meet your colleagues, the cake-eaters from Merrion Square, for instance. There'll be a free bar for two hours. That's like a gilt-edged invitation to get plastered."

Jim was more circumspect. "It's a Christmas social occasion," he said. "Unfortunately, it'll degenerate into a bit of an orgy late in the evening. A free bar, in my view, is always a mistake.

People who normally drink beer will drink brandy or whiskey when they know it's free, and they can't handle it. So they get a bit steamed up. My suggestion for you and Frances is that I take you home before things get to that pitch. Is that all right with you?"

I nodded gratefully.

So next night I found myself sitting with Frances in the big hall in the Hotel Branch. She was a mine of information. "See that swarthy looking man with the big belly and very little hair?"

I looked. "They mostly look like that."

Frances giggled. "No, your man there with the kind of hooded eyes, talking to Tom O'Reilly. That's Frank Purcell, the general secretary. He deals with all staff matters. The man over there with the heavy horn-rimmed glasses, that's Billy McMullen, the general president. He's from Belfast."

"I know him. He rang one day about a strike."

"He's a Protestant, you know, but he goes to all the Catholic funerals and that, no bother. For instance, he was at Tom's funeral the other day. Now, if it were the other way round. . ."

She nodded over to a corner of the room. "That's the head office lot over there. They work over in Merrion Square. You see the way they stick together. They think they're slumming it coming down here to the Hall, but if it wasn't for the members we look after, there'd be no need for them at all."

They looked perfectly ordinary people to me, and, of course, people drifted into little islands of people they knew best. They were more at home there. There was a queue at the bar, and Paddy McLoughlin made his way back with some difficulty, disgorging pints from a tray for the men at his own table and then returning with a drink for Frances, myself and himself.

"God, I'd rather have a drink in a pub of my own choosing," he said. "I hate this kind of thing."

Somebody up at the top table called us to order, and the noise gradually abated as somebody spoke absolutely ineffectively. Nobody could hear a word that was being said.

"Mike, mike," the crowd in front shouted. "We can't hear. Where's Terry?"

Tom O'Reilly made his way to the microphone and tried ineffectively to make it work. His comment, "Jesus, Terry, you've made a hames of this," could be distinctly heard. Everybody laughed and a few ribald remarks were thrown in his general direction.

Terry left the doorway in which he'd been standing and slowly and deliberately made his way to the stage, still in his dungarees, too-big jacket and flat-topped cap. He seemed to be absolutely oblivious to the witticisms thrown in his direction. Somebody up front started the chant "Left, right, left, right, I had a good job and I left, right," in time with his stride, and that caused great merriment. Terry took the microphone in his hands, took a screwdriver out of his pocket, fiddled with it, then breathed into the microphone, the sound like a hurricane.

There was cheering, and jeering, but Terry paid absolutely no attention to that. As he walked away I wondered if by any chance he'd set that up in advance. Certainly he'd upstaged, very publicly, Tom O'Reilly.

The general president, Billy McMullen, was introduced and took his place on the rostrum.

"I'm not one for long speeches," he said, "and certainly not on a night when we can celebrate together the feast that is so closely bound up with peace and brotherhood. But we must remember our dead, those we've lost in this year of 1947. Our thoughts go particularly to Tom, our comrade, laid to rest so recently, and to his family who grieve so terribly for his loss.

"As we remember Tom and all the times we worked together,

let us not forget our other comrades and relatives who have passed on to a better world during 1947. In particular let us remember with pride our executed leader, James Connolly, who went to his death from this building in 1916. Let us remember our dead, comrades, in the usual way."

Everybody stood and raised their glasses in salute. "To our dead comrades."

Then we clinked glasses together within our groups and sat down again.

"Comrades," the general president went on, "as this year of 1947 dwindles to its close, we've all grown older and hopefully wiser together. In two years time we'll be forty years in existence as a union. Before we look to the future, I believe we must look to the past to learn from it.

"In January 1909 Ireland was a corner of a colonial empire. We are now a free, democratic, republican state, at least this side of the border. We have survived much as a union. We have gone through the rigours of the Dublin Lock-out of 1913, the Bloody Sunday massacre, the 1916 rebellion and the death of our leader, James Connolly. We've gone through the bloodiness of the Civil War when brother killed brother. We've seen an Irish state set up, democratic procedures put in train. We've seen the hell of a World War as a neutral state with all that entails.

"Now after years of being kept in an economic straitjacket by the government, we need economic expansion. We need jobs. We need a decent health service. We need houses. We need more money for workers. We must have job security and a decent life style for the members we represent.

"This union will have to fight for these things as hard as we've ever fought for anything before. Our membership before the 1916 Rising was 5,000 and our cash on hands ninety pounds exactly. After the rebellion our leader was executed, our officials and our members either arrested, scattered or dead, and this building and other union property badly damaged by military action.

"In 1923 we had the court case Jim Larkin took claiming that the rules adopted in his absence in America were not legally correct and that the officers elected under those rules were invalidly elected. Members seceded from this union to go with him into the Workers' Union of Ireland, and relationships have been difficult, to put it mildly, since then.

"However, we've got to get on with the business our members require of us, and that means at times taking difficult decisions.

"Streamlining our administrative resources is one of the things we have to accept as a union. We've got to be a professional organisation, which can effectively do the things it needs to do well, but at the same time we must not lose our humanity and our ability to empathise with our members. They are our strength, our reason for existence. We must not lose sight of that truth ever, comrades. Trying to get that balance right is going to be difficult, a balance between being efficient and professional in doing our business and yet being ever aware of the entitlements of the members we represent in human terms.

"And, of course, as employees of the union we too have certain rights as well as certain obligations. One of the areas the national executive council is concerned about is the environment in which many of you work.

"We know that many instances can be put forward of less than acceptable working conditions, not only here in Liberty Hall, but also around the country generally. We realise that the deficiencies must be put right, but, as always, we have to watch our expenditure very carefully. And we have decided, in theory, to begin that process by rebuilding Liberty Hall here on this site."

There was a gasp, then a burst of chatter as people realised the significance of what had been said.

"Yes," the general president continued. "We intend to set up a fund to finance the rebuilding of Liberty Hall on this site. We must always remember that our docker members paid for the repairs to Liberty Hall after 1916 when this building was a shambles. They ceded their first week's wage increase to the ITGWU to get the work done and make a HQ for our union. That was an act of faith that we must always bear in mind. It was also a huge sacrifice in human terms for an ideal of ordinary working men with families and commitments. Men who could quite easily turn their backs on a union that was barely able to function at that time.

"We now intend to build a new modern building here on this site in which our jobs can be done effectively in a deal more comfort than this dilapidated building affords. So, on behalf of the officers and national executive council of the union, I ask you to rise and honour in toast: the Irish Transport and General Workers' Union."

Again everybody stood and raised their glasses. "To the Irish Transport and General Workers' Union," we murmured and clinked our glasses.

I was about to sit down when a voice somewhere at the front was raised singing the "Watchword of Labour"—the same song I'd heard at the funeral procession. Everywhere around me the air was filled with the singing, particularly the "Send it aloft on the breeze, boys!" lines of the chorus.

Even Frances, standing beside me, was singing her heart out. Catching my eye, she whispered, "I'll type out the words if you want. We sing it on all formal occasions."

"I better learn it so," I nodded, "now I'm permanent." And we sat back down again. The main topic of conversation was the proposal to rebuild Liberty Hall. I could hear Tommy McCarthy's group moaning about their own premises in the country, which were in an even worse state than the one we were in.

Frances nodded towards them. "Cork," she said. "The Republic of Cork. They're always whinging." Then she turned away to talk to someone else. I looked about me. The hall was quite full now with people all around in animated conversation. But there were so few women. Frances and myself, the clerical people from head office, Sadie, Peg O'Donnell, Rosie and Nellie, a few women clustered together who probably worked for Tom O'Reilly and other branches at the front of the building, but that was all.

Frances gave me a nudge. "Checking on the talent?" she giggled. "Not that there's much, I'll grant you that."

"There are so few women," I said. "It's surprising, that's all."

"Not to one who has worked awhile here," she replied. "It's the branch secretaries are the power. And they're all men. They generate the income, you see. We sit behind the typewriter or the switchboard. That's all we do. We don't count."

Food began to appear, carried in by some of the people I'd seen in Frances's branch. I looked at her in surprise.

"Our members," she nodded. "After all, it is a union function. Who else would you get?"

Soon our table was laden with dishes, plates of cold roast beef, chicken and ham, salads, bread rolls and soup. Paddy McLoughlin caught my eye and winked.

"We've got ourselves at the right table," he laughed. "When grub is going, always sit at the Hotel Branch table and you'll be looked after."

"Eat up," Frances said. "The dessert's lovely. And there's never enough to go around. So don't dawdle."

As more stuff arrived the table got congested, and a woman and myself lifted the dishes to take them into the kitchen to make way for the tea and coffee that was to follow the dessert.

Frances pulled me back. "No, May, don't do that. It's insulting to the staff. Waiting on table is their trade. They've spent years learning their craft. They want to do it right. Give them their dignity. They deserve it."

I sat back very surprised. "I only. . ."

"I know. But that man. . ." she gestured to a silver-haired man carrying plates right up his arm to his shoulder, "Marcus there, he's an experienced silver-service waiter who's worked in the best hotels in the world. He came home from the Dorchester Hotel in London because his wife was terminally ill. We have some of the best chefs and waiting staff in the world here in Ireland, but we undervalue them just because they do a service job. And they have their pride."

I sat back and watched as the waiting staff got on with their work, very efficiently, but with banter and friendliness as well.

Frances in particular got her fair share of quips and jokes from her branch members, but she responded with wit and good humour. Replete, we took tea or coffee or a drink to finish our meal and chatted and shared experiences with those around us. Paddy came back with a tray of drinks.

"The '*Ta-sê's*' are tuning up," he remarked to Frances, nodding to the stage. "It's the diddley-do music for us tonight."

Indeed three men were unpacking instruments, checking the microphone and placing chairs on the stage.

"Jesus, wouldn't you think they'd get a decent band you could dance to," Frances said disconsolately. "It's going to be another night of '*Ochón is Ochón Ó*'."

It was céilí music all right, and Frances and some fellow called Owen went on and on about the show bands and the dance halls they favoured, while the noise levels in the hall just increased to drown out the music.

Then a man came to the microphone. "Comrades," he said, "now for the noble call. You all know what that means. I'll start the ball rolling with an auld song, then I'll pass the noble call to a colleague of my choosing. And nobody, but nobody, can refuse the noble call. That clear?"

He started off with "On the One Road" to a background of foot tapping, handclapping and back slapping, putting his all into the song. Then he called on another man who sang "The West's Awake" with dramatic gestures and an over-the-top finale. And so it went on. The standard was varied and only two women contributed, Sadie being one.

As the glasses were emptied and refilled, the atmosphere became more and more friendly, with men having emotional reunions, arms draped around each other's shoulders, and insults and jibes traded.

"Wasn't he in your office?" I asked Frances, nodding to a man called on stage to do his bit.

"Ah yeah, that's Mickey Mullen. He'll be a general officer one of these days," Frances said. "At least that's what he thinks. Though your Jumbo might beat him to the punch."

I looked at her in surprise. "You mean Jim might. . ."

We were hushed by those around us as the man began to sing Brendan Behan's "The Auld Triangle" to tapping feet and with everybody joining lustily in the "jingle-jangle" chorus. He got a good reception, with groups on their feet calling for an encore. But he gave the noble call to his colleague Mick Q, took his bow and left the stage.

"That's one cute hoor," a man in front said loudly but was hushed by his companions. Frances pretended not to have heard the remark.

A man was making his way bashfully to the stage through a barrage of good-natured jeering. I looked again. Yes, he was the man I'd seen in the Hotel Branch doing registers like mine. But his army had been in disarray, no way as disciplined as mine.

"Isn't that. . .?" I spluttered to Frances.

"Yeah. He works in our branch. Now wait till you hear his party piece."

He was a big heavy man with a fringe of white hair, heavy-framed glasses and a look of jollity about him. As he stood on the stage he looked sheepish, eyes on the floor, hands clasped in front, shuffling his feet in his embarrassment at finding himself in this position. There were whistles and catcalls and a good-humoured rousting from the audience, and he played along with it like a veteran, looking just like a boy forced to stand shyly in front of the class. He cleared his throat, shuffled his feet, opened his mouth, closed it again, gazed appealingly at the musicians, and then started again.

"The Piddling Pup," he declaimed, in tones of mangled elocution, "a recitation by Michael Quigley." The essence of the recitation was the trials of a pup as he learned the dos and don'ts of where to piddle and how, as learned from an adult dog. The words were amusing, but it was how he struggled to remember the words, the facial expressions and the gestures that went with every line that made the audience rise to its feet and cheer him. Frances was on her feet, arm wrapped around my neck, whooping with delight.

"Didn't I tell you? Isn't that something?" she yelled in my ear as Mick made his way back to his table to wild applause. It was the incongruity that was the key, I thought. This soberly suited, conservative, elderly man parading before us as a worried child doing his best with a piece learned at elocution class by heart and not knowing at all how it would appear to his audience.

I felt a touch on my shoulder and Jim Gilhooley bent down. "I'm ready to go if you ladies are," he said mildly. "Sadie's already in the car and maybe it's a good time to go home."

Frances protested that the night was young, but I was ready to go, and with a bad grace on her part, we said our goodbyes and left with Jim. Sadie sat in the front seat; Frances and I shared the back, and she moaned all the way up to Cabra about how much better it would have been if a bit of dancing had been thrown in.

As we crossed O'Connell Bridge going back to the south side of the city, Jim asked how I'd enjoyed the night. I thought for a moment. "I don't know really. I mean, I've never been at anything like that so I'm no judge. But I thought it'd be more formal, you know, everybody. . ." I didn't know how to finish the sentence.

"M'm, yes. Well, it's a mixed bag really. Staff, mainly Dublin-based with a few from Cork, Limerick and Galway who happened to be present at some conference or something. And, of course, the yes-men who make it their business to be seen at things like that. The point about the dancing that Frances made, well, it's valid in a way. You see, we cling to the old ways, the ways we know, that were there when we came into the movement. But the old ways are going out, new ways replacing them, and really we have to look to the future far more than the past."

"And rebuilding Liberty Hall?"

"That was a bit of a bombshell. But, of course, Billy was only marking our cards on what was in the wind. The NEC recommendation will go to the Annual Delegate Conference, and the members will decide whether or not to go along with it. The financial implications are pretty scary. We can't go to the banks or we'd be in their pockets. So we'll have to raise the cost of rebuilding from our own resources, and that means members paying a voluntary levy over and above their union subs. Even if they agree, it'll take years to accumulate enough money to even get the foundations dug. So we won't be moving into this modern new building next week."

CHAPTER TWENTY-ONE

NEXT MORNING IN our house things were pretty chaotic. I overslept for a start, despite my mother's repeated calls, "Would you ever get up, May?" I only wanted a cup of tea and a slice of bread, but she pushed a dish of porridge under my nose.

"Ye weren't drinking last night, I hope," she said with a bit of a sniff. I looked at her, still bleary-eyed.

"No, I wasn't. But I had three glasses of orangeade, and all that fancy food. . ." I looked resolutely away from the porridge. "But it was good fun!"

"And now you're paying for it," she laughed. "That's the way of the world."

"Well. . . where's everyone?"

"Ger's gone to work, and so is Eileen. Kate is going over her spelling in front of the range before school. Your da's on the post, God love him. Con's not in yet. He's running late if he wants to go to school."

She checked the clock with a worried look. "Kevin's supposed to be still in bed, but I suppose he's hanging out the window to watch the kids go to school."

I too looked at the clock, knowing I'd be dead late for work. Con's early morning stint delivering milk in the neighbourhood was a real penance at this time of year. The milkman he went with, Jude, was overfond of the whiskey bottle. Over-indulgence made his moods unpredictable, but his temper could be even worse when he had none.

Con clattered in at this point, cap crushed down on his head, muffler up around his nose, coat collar turned up, his hands clasped under his armpits to relieve the pain. Delivering milk in glass bottles to the doorsteps before dawn in this cold frosty weather was not for the faint-hearted.

"Jesus! Oh Mother of God, it's cold out!" He stood white-faced in front of the range trying to get the heat back into his bones.

My mother took his cap and muffler off and sat him down in front of the range, opening its innards to let the heat out more quickly. She handed him a mug of hot tea, but he couldn't hold the mug in his blue and numbed hands. She held the mug to his lips.

"Come on, Con. Just swallow a little, little sips. Take your time. That's the ticket." She smoothed his hair back from his face, holding him close to her. "Come on, Con. That's my baby."

As the numbness passed, the shivering got worse. She handed me the mug.

"Get him to swallow little sips. Keep at him. I'll be back in a minute."

She came back with a blanket and wound it around Con. She dipped his hands in a basin of warm water and then rubbed them quickly with a towel. He squirmed with pain, his head turned away from us. She knelt and took off his boots and stockings and started to rub his feet with the towel. "Just keep giving him the tea," she said. "We've got to get the blood circulating."

Con was weeping, but trying desperately not to be seen to be a cry-baby. I was close to tears myself, and I knew my mother was too. Gradually things eased. I got a fresh mug of tea and Con managed to drink it himself. Then he demolished a dish of porridge and two slices of bread, and began to worry about going to school.

"Maybe you'd give it a miss today," my mother suggested. "It's the last day before the holidays. You could lie beside Kevin. He'd be glad of the company."

But Con was adamant. He had to go to school. The last day before the holidays was so looked forward to, and he wanted to savour it. My mother watched him from the doorway as he trotted off down the road, head bent, muffled up in coat, cap and scarf, his smoke-like breath drifting behind him.

As I passed her on my way to catch the bus to work, she put her hand on my shoulder. "Sorry if I was a bit quick on the draw earlier. It's just you were so late in, and I was awake waiting. I couldn't sleep. It was the first time you were out on your own. Well, you know how it is."

"Yeah, I know. And everything's coming together, all the worries. You'd never think the season of peace and goodwill was around the corner." We touched hands briefly in a gesture of mutual understanding. "But, please God, things will look up soon, Ma. See you later."

In the office, I ignored Sadie's pointed look at the clock and concentrated on the list of work taped to the wall. All the work we'd done was ticked off, but it seemed to me that an awful lot remained to be done, and this was now three days before Christmas.

Jim stood behind me. "We've a bit of leeway, you know. It's not as bad as it looks. The firms won't start back until the New Year, and even then they won't be at full strength. So we'll get a clear run in the few days after Christmas. So don't you worry about it."

I hoped he was right, but I had my doubts. I sat at my desk

and started again the interminable job of writing names into the register, then from it writing the new shop stewards' books, ticking-off the completed work on the master sheet.

Paddy put his head around the door. "Now hear this, now hear this," he said, his fingers closing his nostrils in an imitation of an American film captain making an announcement over the tannoy to his crew. "The admiral has instructed all crew to assemble in the prow of the ship at 17.00 hours. Those who fail to show will walk the plank at dawn tomorrow. That is all."

"Quit the messing, Paddy," I said. "What's all that about?"

Sadie, Jim and myself all looked at Paddy in mystification.

"Whatever it is, I can't go," Jim said after a look at his diary. "That meeting in Smyth's entails waiting for the night workers to come in. God knows what time I'll get out of there."

Sadie murmured something about five o'clock being a crazy time for anything to be arranged a few days before Christmas and that she wouldn't be there either.

Paddy rolled his eyes to heaven. "Mutiny!" he exclaimed. "The crew are asking why. I don't know what the world is coming to. Sure, you never do that with an admiral. You just say, 'Aye, aye, sir.' You lot will end up feeding the crabs, mark my words." He went off chuckling without further explanation. We went back to our work, Jim later drifting away to Frank Robbins to find out what was the explanation for this five o'clock call-out.

"It's the band," Jim said, back and warming his rear at the fire. "A group of port members were putting on a show for the hospital in Baldoyle this evening. But the electricity is off in the hall they were to use, and they couldn't get another at this late stage. And now, the acts they intended to put on have just pulled out, leaving them hanging there. So they asked Terry could we do something. The big Hotel Branch hall is out because there's a do on there tonight. So it's to be in the front hall instead."

Sadie snorted in disbelief.

"That's not the best of an arrangement I agree, but it's all that can be done at the last minute. Tom O'Reilly pulled the band in to hold the thing together. They were rehearsing for that gig for the Lord Mayor over in the Mansion House, and so it's been decided to put on a Christmas carol concert here in the hall before the band's normal rehearsal. The whole idea is to help the children's hospital out in Baldoyle. The port members hope they'll collect a few bob for them, and fair play to them for trying."

"What band?" I asked, thinking it must be some showband.

"The union band, of course," Jim said, taking his wallet out and looking at its contents thoughtfully. "Brass and reed. They're quite good actually. They've won international competitions for military bands."

"A military band?" That seemed to me to be such a crazy idea that I couldn't hide my disbelief.

"In keeping with our past," Jim laughed. "Of course, you've never really seen the band in action, and maybe this is your chance. Can I impose on you again, May? You see, I think it's a good idea for the union to be involved in community affairs, and I know the hospital needs funds desperately. But I can't be here, so I wonder if you. . .?"

"Would act on your behalf? Sure, if that's OK."

Jim pulled a fiver out of his wallet and stuck it in a sealed envelope, writing his name and "'Clothing Branch—ITGWU" on it, then handing it to me. "They'll have a bucket collection, so you just throw it in when the opportunity comes." I put it away carefully.

"Now, there are a couple of things I wanted to say to you, May. I never seem to get the time to do it properly. First off, no working late tonight. OK? You do this job for me and we'll do our stint tonight without you. Fair is fair. And you don't have to work on Christmas Eve. It generally turns into a bit of a drinking session, and it's no place for you. Or me either, if it comes to that! But it's part of my job and I must do it.

"I haven't been able to give you the time off you're due. I'm conscious of that, but hopefully we'll make it up in the New Year. So we'll resume the day after St Stephen's Day. We have to get back early to try to get the paperwork done. I give you my word that I'll make sure you're compensated for the extra hours you've put in. OK?"

I nodded and Jim began to shrug into his coat.

"Oh, and one more thing. I'll be driving out to Blackrock tomorrow at lunchtime to collect the union money, and if you want to take home some Christmas stuff, I could drop you home on the way. I can't say what time I'd be coming back, but it'd save you carrying stuff on the bus. Oh, and Rosie asked me to remind you about the biscuits she has for you."

I looked at the press where I'd been allocated some space for my things. There were two bags there already. It'd be a great help not to have to lug the stuff home on the bus, but there was another thing worrying me.

"Thanks, Jim," I said gratefully, "but. . ."

Jim stopped in the doorway. "What is it, child?"

"This collection for the hospital. . .I can't. . ."

"Nor would you be expected to," Jim said firmly. "My envelope is from the branch, from all of us. No individual contributions—that'd be out of order." He smiled and was gone.

At around 4.45 p.m. I began to tidy things away, making sure the fires were stoked up and getting things ready for those who'd work later. Coat on, envelope safely in my pocket, I turned outside the office door to go down the corridor to the front of the building.

A bit of plywood had been put across the entry with a "No Entry" sign attached, with the paint dripping down and the wording slanting clearly to the left. As I looked, a man came towards me along the corridor, which was even gloomier than usual. He was dressed in dark dungarees, an old tweedy sports jacket, muffler pulled high around his neck, cap pulled firmly down on his head, smoking a cigarette. And he was black!

I stood transfixed. It was only when he stood at the other side of the barrier that I realised that he was actually a white man but black from oil or something.

He touched his cap in a salute.

"Excuse me, Miss, is Sean boy in?" he asked with a Cork lilt. "What?"

The man smiled. "Is it me Cork accent you don't understand? I'm looking for Sean, the secretary of the Railroad Branch of the union. He works in there." He pointed at a door in the corridor opposite to Tommy McCarthy's office.

"I don't know. I've worked here a few weeks and never seen anyone in there. I don't even know what he looks like."

"Once seen, never forgotten. Ah well, most times Sean's somewhere on the rail network. It stands to reason as that's where his members are. Me now, I'm a fireman on the plate. You see, it's me break time and I didn't have time to make meself presentable for the female sex! I've got to get back now; trains wait for no man. Would you tell him Jobe Corr was looking for him and it's fairly urgent. OK?"

I wrote his name down on the back of a receipt in my pocket to remind myself to deal with the message, and he went off with a flip of the hand and a "See you".

If Ger got the rail job he would be like Jobe. It bore some thinking about.

When I got down to the door on to the quay, I stopped in

amazement. It was snowing! Maybe we'd have a white Christmas after all. I pulled my coat collar up and buckled my belt tighter, then looked down at my shoes. They were new, well, not exactly new. My mother had done some kind of deal. I didn't know the details, nor did I want to know. At least the shoes were waterproof, even though they still hadn't settled into the shape of my feet, nor probably ever would.

I stepped out into the snowstorm with the wind driving the snow down the river right into my face. Outside the Hotel Branch doorway, I paused as I heard Frances's voice shouting back something to those inside.

"No, I won't be back. I'm bloody freezing. I'm going for a hot whiskey after this, so don't bother me." She paused in the doorway to put up her umbrella.

"Damned stupid, that's what I am. Going to a bleedin' carol concert in a freezing kip like Liberty Hall, while the snow pours down out of the heavens. May, don't say anything to me about it being a white Christmas or I swear to God I'll run you through with this umbrella!"

We laughed together and she took my arm as she tapped along on her high heels to the corner of Beresford Place. Again I wondered at how she managed to keep her balance in the slushy street on those heels.

"Jesus! I don't believe it! That gobshite Terry's shut the bloody front door. Would you believe it?"

I gaped around the umbrella to see what she meant. It was true. About thirty or forty people were grouped around the entrance to Liberty Hall, and the big door was firmly shut fast.

"I don't believe it!"

"It's true, missus." A man with his head burrowed down in his coat collar like a tortoise, hands thrust down into his pockets, turned around, his face blue with the cold. "It was shut when we got here. Would they have gone home? Forgotten, maybe?"

"I'll sort this out," Frances said, her voice cutting like a knife. "Let me through. Jesus, Terry, if I get my hands on you. . ."

She pushed her way through the crowd, all heads turning to watch as she made for the doorway. "Terry, open the bloody door. It's freezing out here. What in the name of God do you think you're doing?"

She rapped sharply on the door with the handle of her umbrella. "Terry, stop acting the gobshite. Open the door or I swear to God I'll kill you with my own bare hands."

A voice, not Terry's, answered. "Ah, would you ever hold your patience, missus. Things are a bit chaotic in here. The fuses are all gone and we're doing the best we can. It's black dark in here."

In the silence that followed, several voices could be heard distinctly from inside the door.

"Jackie, would you ever keep that light steady."

"Jesus, how can I see anything when you set your big arse right in my way."

"We should have. . ."

"Say that one more time and I swear to God I'll. . ."

Then Tom O'Reilly's voice. I'd know it anywhere.

"Folks, sorry for the mishap. We'll be ready to open up in about two minutes."

"I suppose the band's gone home for its tea," a woman's voice in the front said. "I wish to Christ I'd done the same. I'm famished as well as frozen."

"The band," a man in front of me spoke. "Sure they're probably marching down along Ballybough. I see them do that two nights a week. Sure, they've to practise their marching for that marching band competition."

"Marching, them? You must be joking!"

That was a tall, thin woman with a coat over her head to protect her from the snow. "The Sufferin' Ducks! Sure, God Almighty, they do be puce in the face after the first fifty yards. As for the poor fellow with the big drum, sure your heart would go out to him. The sweat does be dripping off him like water down a waterfall."

There was a titter amongst the crowd. I stood on tiptoes to see where Frances had gone. She was still battering on the door and shouting to them to "Open the bloody door." I felt my belt grasped from behind, and I was pushed back against the railings.

"Hey, young one. Where do you think you're going?"

I squirmed around to see who was doing it.

"What. . .?"

"Just to let you know you can't walk through me."

The woman was big, maybe an inch taller than me but big in every way, a man's gaberdine coat around her shoulders, a wet scarf over hair that was wiry and tough, fat rosy cheeks and flesh that seemed to escape from the clothes she wore with absolute abandon.

"What. . ."

"Ye've elbows, young one, that could peel spuds they're so sharp," the woman said. "Keep them to yourself, there's a good girl."

"I didn't. . ."

"You won't. So that's settled. My name's Abina. What's yours?"

"May."

"Born in May, were you?"

"Yeah." This conversation was so foolish I could hardly believe it. The door opening made a welcome diversion.

"Take your time now." That was Tom O'Reilly again.

The crowd surged forward and jammed in the doorway.

"Jesus, they're all wanting to pay their union dues, Tom." That was Tommy McCarthy.

There was a titter of laughter amongst the crowd as we filed in, glad to be out of the blast of the biting wind. Spotting me, Frances waved me over to her side and we perched together on a ballot box laid on its side. Abina, to my astonishment, followed me. A man, looking at her size with disbelief, came back with a high-backed chair, and it was handed over the heads of the crowd and room made so she could sit in it.

"Connolly's own chair," Tommy McCarthy said. "You're privileged, m'am."

I looked around me with astonishment. The lights were minimal, the seats anything that could be used, even a ladder placed against the back wall with people perched along its length. The entry to the corridor was gone, covered by something dark. Tom O'Reilly thanked us for coming and apologised for the delay in letting us in, particularly with the weather as harsh as it was and the disappointment about the other hall. He then said, "Over to you, Terry."

The figure of Terry, obvious even in the dimness, bent and pulled a switch or something, and suddenly there was a fairytale lighted Christmas Tree.

There was a concerted drawing of breaths, "Ah's" and "God, will you look at that!"

From the stairway in semi-darkness, a group of uniformed men delivered a fanfare of trumpets. The sound of the silvery instruments soared up into the darkened building. I know I jumped a couple of inches off my seat, as did Frances, and most of the audience, at the suddenness of the sound.

They began to play "Winter Wonderland", "White Christmas" and so on in a Christmas medley. As they played, the kids in the audience were lifted to sit in the front on a piece of old carpet, and boxes of sweets were handed around.

"Silent Night" followed, sung to an attentive audience by a boy soprano, who ended on a high note to generous applause.

"He's from the Palistrina, you know, the boys from the Pro-Cathedral." Abina nudged me. "It's beautiful, isn't it? I wonder if they have anybody from the Rathmines and Rathgar?"

I gaped at her, not knowing at all what she meant.

As if in answer, "Now we're going up-market," Tom said. "A nice little piece from *Maritana* sung by a few stalwart members who happen also to be members of the Rathmines and Rathgar Choral Society. A piece known to most of us as 'Angels that Around Us Hover'. Please honour our musicians by your attention."

"What'd I tell you," Abina said, clapping vigorously. "The Rathmines and Rathgar are really the best around. Now, when you've got good soloists and a full choir, God it's great stuff! Those operettas, there's nothing like them. But those soloists did well, so they did."

Frances playfully punched my arm. "Who's your friend? I think she fancies you!" She went into a fit of giggles.

I looked at her, only half understanding what she meant.

"But. . ." I spluttered, "it's only. . ."

"Hush!" Abina suddenly loomed over me, her bulk a bit intimidating. "Have you no respect for the performers? I'm ashamed of you!"

Dutifully I looked up front to where a drummer dressed in a tunic with striped trousers and a military cap stood with drum-sticks poised, ready to accompany the boy soprano in "The Little Drummer Boy".

As they got under way a woman in front leaned back to Abina to whisper, "That's my youngest, the young lad with the drum.

Sure, he's mad about music. He drives us round the bend prac-
tising. But the union band has been great for him; it's opened
so many doors. He's a little dote isn't he?"

Abina patted her shoulder. "He's just gorgeous. A little angel.
Will you look at him, playing away there for the Blessed Infant.
You must be a proud mother this day."

Totally unabashed by the disapproving glares turned on her,
she began to root amongst the clothes draped across her knees,
her chair creaking alarmingly. Eventually she produced a brown
paper bag of bull's-eyes, the black-striped boiled sweets stuck
together and requiring dextrous manipulation as she offered
the bag to all around her. Soon we all had bulging cheeks, and
the pungent peppermint smell wafted all round us, defeating
the musty smell of wet clothes and decaying building.

"Bravo," she shouted, clapping vigorously as the lads finished
and took their bows. She slapped the back of the woman in front
so hard in congratulation that she nearly fell off her precarious
seat on a tea box.

Tom was back. "Now, folks, we're coming towards the interval
when we'll send a bucket around for the collection for the Children's Hospital. I want to hear a good ould cheerful jangle as it
goes its rounds.

"We'll end this half of the concert with a Christmas medley
from the band. We all know these songs, so let's raise the roof
so that Santa can hear us!"

The dim lights hit off the shiny musical instruments as they
were raised. Then on the lifting of the conductor's baton, we
were off, with Abina beside me leading us all in "Jingle Bells",
then "Good King Wenceslas" and "Away in the Manger", and
having a go at "Adeste Fideles".

As the men put down their instruments, and Tom prepared to
declare the interval, a man stood up and faced us. He still wore

his army surplus greatcoat, which being wet must have weighed a ton. I got the impression that what he wore under it was not, perhaps, in his terms, respectable enough for the company.

"Can I. . .I'm only a labourer from Mayo. Not trained or educated or that. This time of year. . .away from home too long. It'd make my Christmas if I could sing an old traditional Christmas lullaby from my part of the world, *"Codail a Linbh"*. If that's all right?"

He waited and Tom gave him the nod. "I'll give you a couple of English lines first, otherwise you won't know what's meant." Leaning against the wall he spoke in the soft lilt of Mayo just a little above a whisper.

> "I worship my little child come on earth,
> Sleep peacefully, my child,
> Tell me, my love, as you lie in the manger,
> Tell me why you lie stretched in the straw,
> You are a treasury of grace, Jesus Son of God."

Then his voice was lifted in song, soft and gentle, filled with an inexpressible sorrow, as the Irish words of the lullaby filled the darkened space. As the sound drifted away there was a moment of silence before the applause broke it.

As it ceased, Abina raised her voice in a solo rendering of "Oh Holy Night". The band members belatedly providing an improvised backing. It was extraordinary. Her voice was powerful, controlled, at ease with the very difficult requirements of that hymn, no easy thing as I knew from the school choir. When the last high note soared, there was a standing ovation for her performance, including from the bandsmen.

Tom, applauding her himself, said simply, "To try to follow those two last performances would be an obscenity. So we'll take that break now."

Curious about the blocked corridor, I craned my neck to see what had been done now that my eyes had adjusted to the semi-darkness. Behind the tree where the corridor should be was what looked like the front wall of a cottage with lighted windows, a half-door and a little chimney on top. Descending into that chimney was Santa Claus with a bulging sack. I gaped at it, not believing what I was seeing. Standing beside it, Terry puffed away at his pipe, not a bother on him. Catching my eye he grinned and lifted his pipe in salute.

Frances leaned past me and stuck her hand out towards Abina. "I'm Frances. I'd be waiting a long time for your woman here to introduce us."

They shook hands. "Abina, that's me," Abina said. "Are you friends?"

"Yeah, we work together here in the hall. You've a beautiful voice, Abina. That 'Oh Holy Night' was really something. Do you sing publicly, in choirs or whatever?"

Abina settled herself more comfortably, the chair protesting audibly. "Thanks, girl. No, I don't sing, just around the house, or at a family do or something or maybe in the pub, after the stalls are cleaned off and folded away. I'm a trader in Moore Street just like my mother before me, ye see, and when you've stood at your stall all day in weather like this, believe me it's a treat to get in anywhere out of the cold. If an ould bar of a song can raise the spirits, then Abina's in her alley."

The man from Mayo approached, sunk into the army great-coat, his hands in his pockets. Abina beckoned him forward. "Come here, son. I'd like a word with you." We squeezed up to make room for him. He was tall and thin, with lank black hair that badly needed cutting, and he also needed a shave.

He spoke to Abina without really looking at her. "Yes, m'am. You wanted me?"

"Yes. I wanted to ask you about that lullaby. It was beautiful. I've no Irish myself. I've sold stuff on the streets here in Dublin since I was eight. I never learned Irish. When I heard you sing like that, I regretted not knowing it more than ever. Tell me now, would you sing it at midnight mass at home or what?"

"When we'd be walking to midnight mass, and coming back too. That and others, other Christmas things in the Gaelic. You'd hear the singing in the black darkness and you'd know you weren't alone. Others would be on the road too, next to you and far from you, and you'd hear it coming back from the stones of the road."

Abina held out her hand and the man reached out his, a hand scarred and calloused, with black and broken nails. "You've made this woman very happy," she said gently. "I only raised my voice in that hymn to soften the hurt for you."

"You've made this man very happy too. Your singing was glorious. I'm privileged to have preceded you. I'd never have had the temerity to have followed you." The man smiled, looking Abina eye to eye.

Suddenly I realised how attractive he was, a bit like Gregory Peck down on his luck. Abina rooted in the pocket of the coat on her lap. "Allow me to give you a little gift in honour of the occasion," she said, handing him a paper bag. "It's only a bag of broken chocolate," she said regretfully, "but it's given with a heart and a half." She leaned forward and kissed him on the cheek.

"And it's accepted with sincere gratitude by this Mayo man," he said. "Happy Christmas, m'am, to you and yours."

"May Christ be with you," Abina said, and the man moved off.

The band then launched into a medley of marching tunes that soon had all toes tapping on the floor. Tom conferred with a little nondescript man in a woolly Aran jumper, which seemed to have been made for a man far bigger than he was. Tom got him unwillingly standing beside him, then announced, "Christy Flynn, my good friend Christy Flynn, has now been persuaded to favour us with a recitation.

"I've tried to prevail on him to give us one of his own poems, but he's unwilling to do so. He says he's not ready yet, but he will give us a poem written by Robert Frost entitled 'Acquainted with the Night'. The title is particularly apt because Christy is a Dublin Corpo nightwatchman minding the Corpo stuff up in Aungier Street. He certainly is acquainted with the night. Over to you, Christy."

The man stood before us like a loosely held puppet, pale watery eyes, strings of hair combed over to cover the bald patch, wringing his hands together as though he was drying them.

He coughed, cleared his throat, and then spoke.

"'Acquainted with the Night', written by Robert Frost."

His voice was mellow and fruity, a bit like the bishop when he'd come to our church to confirm us, or like an actor, James Mason, maybe. Totally different from what you'd expect.

> "I have been one acquainted with the night.
> I have walked out in rain—and back in rain.
> I have outwalked the furtherest city light.
> I have looked down the saddest city lane.
> I have passed the watchman on his beat
> And dropped my eyes, unwilling to explain.
> I have stood still and stopped the sound of feet
> When far away an interrupted cry
> Came over houses from another street
> But not to call me back or say goodbye;
> And further still at an unearthly height,
> One luminous clock against the sky
> Proclaimed the time was neither wrong nor right.
> I have been one acquainted with the night."

There was a silence when the man finished speaking and he stood, a puppet with nobody to move him. Then there was thunderous applause, and he went bemused back to his seat, escorted by Tom. When it was all over and Tom had said his thanks to all concerned, it was a quarter past six and outside was grey, frosty, and cold and extremely unwelcoming.

"Come into Barney's and get a hot whiskey," Frances said to both Abina and myself. "The gang will be there. There'll be a bit of gas."

I declined on the excuse of things I needed to do at home, Abina saying she'd a ten-month old girl to see to at home and she'd be driving the rest of the tenants in the flats mad yelling for her grub. She layered herself back into her various coats, leaned across and gave us both a hug, exhorting us to remember to look out for her when next we were in Moore Street.

My bus, when eventually it came, slithered and slid its way through streets that seemed alien in their coating of snow.

"Watch your step there, child," the busman advised as I stepped down from the platform. "It's treacherous, black ice under a thin layer of snow. It'd be easy to break an ankle."

I made my way carefully home through silent white streets with the evening's music still drifting around the back of my mind.

At home it was bright, warm, with a delicious smell I knew well drifting out the front door when I opened it. "Apple dumpling," I grinned to myself, Con's favourite dish. We had the dumpling for afters, its crusty top rising high over the sides of the dish, the dough supported by the hen egg-cup, Kevin's favourite, smelling deliciously of cooked apple, cloves, cinnamon and caramelised sugar, and beside it a jug of yellow custard, ready to pour.

Con crammed the last scrapings of his plate into his mouth.

"Can I go out for an hour or so, no school, so no homework? We've made the best slide ever out on the hill. And the runners on the sledge are just great. She goes like a rocket!"

My mother looked at him a bit doubtfully. "But it's so cold. And you've an early start. . ."

"Ma, Grumpy Gertie will probably be out tomorrow throwing ashes on our lovely slide. It'll be ruined. And it's perfect today."

Kate and Kevin were tugging at Con. "Can I go too?" "Please, Con, can I have a go?" "Me too."

"It's too cold," my mother said half-heartedly.

Con read the signs. "For half an hour, maybe. I'd be very careful of them. Honest to God."

"Well, dress up warm. Half an hour only. And, Con, don't let Kevin stand around in the cold. His ould lungs are a bit delicate."

Off they went with Con, feet barely touching the ground in their excitement.

My mother sighed. "It takes so little to make them happy. But I hope Con keeps his eye on Kevin. A chill now could be a disaster for the little man."

We cleared away the tea things and began the wash-up.

"After tomorrow I'm off work," I said. "I haven't to work on Christmas Eve and I'm not back till the day after Stephen's Day. Jim said he'd drop me off at the top of the road tomorrow with any Christmas stuff I'd to bring home. I've to collect a box of biscuits from the shop and I've a few bits and pieces for the kids. And Da's slippers. We've a lovely present for you, but you can't see it till Christmas Day."

"Well, well, being left home by car. Doesn't that beat Banaher." My mother dried her hands on the towel. "But you didn't see what Con brought in."

She opened the backdoor and we both looked out. There, placed neatly on a sack, was a pile of holly, red berries gleaming, and tendrils of ivy twined through it. "He carried it in a sack on his back down from the golf club. There is enough for Abbie and us, he said. And, May, you'd want to see his hands! They're in bits, torn and gashed, with broken nails, the lot. We'll start the decorating when the kids come in. They like to be involved in making Christmas work."

The kids came in shortly afterwards, cold, bone-tired, but thrilled beyond words at being out in the starry snow-blurred world. And the slide! It was the greatest experience imaginable, flying like a bird with the whoosh of the earth rushing by.

By the time we'd decorated the house, after despatching Eileen off to her mother's with their share of the holly, both kids were exhausted. Kevin went off to bed unresistingly for once. Kate stoically finished putting up the decorations, some made by her at school. She put the crib, minus the infant, up on the mantel above the range, and then the red candle in the window awaiting its light till Christmas Eve, before she gave way to her tiredness.

"I've had the bestest day," she said, sipping her cocoa, before getting into bed. "The slide was like being with Santa on his sleigh, flying along above the ground quicker than anything. But, of course, Santa's got the reindeer. They'd never let Santa get a bruise on his bum from the sledge like I did." And with that she was fast asleep.

Con, my mother and I were joined by Ger, who had been visiting a friend in hospital. My mother poured out another mug of tea for him. "Your da'll only have two rounds to do tomorrow," she remarked, offering him the last buttered scone on the plate. "Then two more on Christmas Eve at the worst. So he'll see an end to it soon. But after that. . ."

"Something'll turn up," Ger said hopefully. "When you see the hospital ward and the guys who'd give their right arm just to be at home for Christmas, it puts the thing into perspective. I think we should just thank God for what we have and what we can give the kids to make their Christmas something to remember. Time enough to think about afterwards when it's over."

I told them about my plans, and immediately Con said he'd meet me at the shops on the main road to help carry down the stuff when Jim left me off at lunchtime next day. Both Con and Ger had made a few bob in Christmas tips, and their contribution to the family purse joined my wages. We now had enough funds to have a decent meal on Christmas Day. My father wouldn't be paid off on the post until his stint ended on Christmas Eve. My mother put the purse into her apron pocket with her head downcast and a muttered, "Thanks, kids. I'm sorry. . ."

Con looked at me sideways. "I suppose you're gone beyond having a go on the sledge yourself? Like, being one of the world's permanent workforce, maybe it'd be beneath your dignity?"

That surprised me, but it only took a moment to decide. "I'd love a go. Can I?"

He grinned. "Better make the most of this evening. Grumpy Gertie is probably getting her bucket of ashes ready right at this moment to destroy the slide."

"Be careful. . ." My mother was talking to our backs as we geared up to go out.

"It's a hard black frost," Ger said. "The buses are having a hard time. God, one of them going up the rise over Mount Street bridge began to slip back. All the driver could do was to pray to God he'd hit nothing on his way back down the hill. And on the Long Hill at Glen-o'-the-Downs. . ." But we were gone before he finished.

Outside the roofs and the trees looked like one of those Dickensian Christmas cards, only short of a post chaise pulling up to the door of the inn with snorting horses and a horn fanfare.

We picked our way carefully round to the hill where about twenty kids were gathered around two slides.

"That's the infant slope," Con said, pointing to the shorter one. As we looked, a ramshackle sledge came unstuck, and its three riders went head over heels down the hill till stopped by willing hands from further bruising. He looked at the other, longer slide. "That's the best slide we've ever made," he said with pride.

It was indeed. The hill, its surface seldom used by traffic, went in an S-shaped circuit downhill, with a graduated slope initially leading to a steep drop.

Down below at the railings, kids were placed strategically to stop sledges, or their riders, crashing into the iron public park railings. I hoped they'd be vigilant when it came to our turn.

"Ready to go?" Con asked with raised eyebrow. I nodded and he retrieved his sledge from Jackie and checked its runners expertly before placing it on the ground at the top of the run.

"Now, sit low and tight to me," he advised. "When I shout 'Left' we both lean that way, 'Right' the opposite, and if I shout 'Jump', you jump right. OK?"

If it came to that, there wasn't much choice. To go left would mean hitting the concrete hard with possible broken bones; right meant hitting the frosted grassy mounds of a disused hillock.

"OK—ready, lads?"

We crouched down on the sledge, Con grasping the rope guidelines, and felt the hands on our shoulders and in our ears the wheezing breathing of our pushers-off as we got going. It was as Con had said, perfection! At first we weren't going particularly fast, but our momentum increased greatly after we'd hit the first speed bump that catapulted us at least six inches off the ground. "Left, left," Con shouted, and as one we leaned into the bend, skimming across the glass-smooth slide. I straightened as he did, then "Right, right" and again the same ritual, leaning into the bend to get the maximum speed possible. As the ground beneath us fell away, our speed increased till it was barely possible to breathe, yet all I could hear was the whoosh of the runners beneath us and the almost physical slam of the air we disturbed in passing.

In front Con was screaming, and I was too. Earth and sky and reality were all blurred when eventually willing hands pulled us sideways off the slide at the base.

I tried to stand up but at first my legs failed to obey my commands, and I had to sit for a few minutes to get my breath and get my limbs under control again.

"What'd I tell you?" Con was exuberant. "Isn't it the best ever?"

I agreed wholeheartedly. "Want another go?" he asked, but I refused, knowing it could never be as perfect the second time around. He agreed and handed over his sledge to Jackie for safe-keeping. We walked home cat-footed in a companionable silence.

As we came to our door I paused for a moment. "Con, it was truly perfect. I'll always remember it." And we let ourselves in and crept as noiselessly as we could away to our beds.

CHAPTER TWENTY-TWO

NEXT MORNING I woke up early, aware it was the last day before Christmas Eve. I looked out the window; yes, the snow remained on the roof opposite, and frost had etched its pattern on the glass of the window. Jumping out of bed, I winced as my bare foot hit the cold lino, and then I scrambled quickly into my clothes. Washed, hair brushed, I found my mother in the kitchen on her knees, swearing to herself at the slowness of the range to respond to her bits of sticks and paper, the cinders and the ashes carefully segregated on newspaper.

"Bloody cranky git, that's what you are," she said with venom to the range. "As soon as I've a few bob, you're on your way out, buster. I'll get me a nice neat little marble fireplace with a little low mantelpiece instead. A fire that'll light up no bother as soon as you put a match to it."

The range responded with a belch of smoke, and the little blue flames visibly weakened as though on an order. I took the ashes out and took our usual remedial measures. That meant sticking a few sticks into the can of paraffin oil that stood inside the shed door and wrapping newspaper tightly around each stick.

Ma took the sticks and pushed them gingerly into the diminishing flames. Suddenly there was a whoosh of fire. She built up the fire with coal and turf pieces, and gradually it turned red and some heat was thrown out.

There was a clatter outside the front door.

"Con," she said, as she levered herself back up on her feet. "I'd know his feet anywhere."

It was indeed Con. But a very different Con from the one I'd seen last night. He was panting, sweating, and his clothes were muddied; he'd a scratch on his cheek and a gash on one leg with the blood seeping into the stocking that hung at half-mast down his leg.

"Con!" My mother was on her feet going to him. "God Almighty, Con, what's happened to you?"

He shrugged out of his coat and let his cap and muffler fall to the floor. "I'm OK, Ma. Honest. It's just, Paddy the horse fell. He slipped at the corner at O'Hanlon's; you know, there's a bit of a slope there. And the milk cart, well, its wheel hit the kerb and it tilted and the milk all fell over."

My mother pushed him to a chair at the table and poured tea and buttered bread for him. I handed him my untouched plate of porridge. "Come on, Con. Eat and take a drop of tea. That's the lad. And yourself, were you on the cart?"

Con looked up with a moustache of milk on his lips. "No, Ma. You see, I've to run about three houses in advance of Paddy. He just ambles along, but I've to run up and down the driveways in the avenues. I've to keep in advance of him. I was in Moore's drive when I heard the crash, and I just threw the bottles down and legged it as quick as I could back. God! It was awful to see him threshing around, trying to get back on his feet and so frightened, his mouth all frothy and his eyes rolling back in his head."

"And Jude?"

"I don't know whether he fell or he jumped. He was sitting on the edge of the path with his hands over his head moaning. He didn't seem much hurt."

Con applied himself to the bread and jam in front of him. "But this man, Larry, he was just fantastic. He was in a shop and ran out when he heard the crash. He grabbed a few empty sacks and. . .I was dead scared of Paddy. He was out of his mind with fear and his two front hooves were threshing through the air. You see, a shaft had broken as well as the wheel, and there was no way he could get up. But this man, he just caught the horse's head and pulled him down, talking to him real cool, even with those hooves just inches away.

"Is Paddy dead then?" a voice behind us asked. We all swivelled around. Kate and Kevin stood there, evidently aroused by the drama in Con's voice. "Is he?" Kate persisted, Kevin beside her, his thumb being sucked vigorously. My mother hooshed them back to bed with a promise of toast and a full story from Con for themselves as soon as Con finished his breakfast.

Con pushed back his chair and sat back, my mother watching him anxiously. "You're sure you're all right, Con? That gash on your leg, it needs to be cleaned. And your clothes, that pocket needs a stitch, and there's a couple of buttons missing. And the mud. Leave them with me for an hour or two and I'll do a job on them."

But Con wasn't interested in this. "The last I saw of Paddy was Larry leading him hobbling into Jacob's shed, talking away to him and promising him a nice bucket of oats as soon as he got settled."

"And Jude?"

Con was scornful. "He sat on the kerb moaning about what he'd lost and never even raised a hand to help Paddy. He doesn't deserve to have a horse!"

He went off with a few slices of toast to ease the hunger pangs and two mugs of milky tea, to regale Kate and Kevin with the saga of Paddy's fall.

I stood at the door ready to go to work. "I'll be finished at six. Then it's Christmas!"

My mother came with me to the door. "OK—a sandwich will do, I suppose? Incidentally, Abbie's coming around for the evening, you heard that?"

"No. But. . ."

"Well, Mrs Jennings thought she's got a bit depressed, down in herself. I suppose it's natural enough as she can't do the things she'd normally do at Christmas. She is stuck there and not able to move while Josie does it all. And one of the babies isn't doing all that well either; that's a worry too. Anyway, Mrs Jennings thought a change of scene would do her good. The family intend doing up the room while she's here, a bit of wall-papering and painting, freshening it up.

"So she'll be here from around two. They've borrowed Jordan's wheelchair to bring her around. I hope there won't be a problem because of the snow."

I stood at the bus stop with a motley crowd of people muffled up in coats, scarves, hats and gloves, and watched, with them, the passing traffic and not a bus in sight. Cars, trucks and lorries moved at a snail's pace in convoy. Now and again an injudicious touch on the brakes made one of them sidle sideways on the ice or touch momentarily, or in one case doing a swirl right around. It was fascinating to watch.

"Jesus Christ, have all the buses gone into hibernation?" a man asked angrily. "I've been here nearly twenty minutes and not a sight of one."

Just then a bus came around the corner, nearly invisible with the snow covering it. We all tramped aboard, stamping feet to get rid of the snow first. I found myself sitting beside a thin little woman in a black coat with a scarf over her hair. She had extremely large boots over sparrow-like legs. She took out her rosary beads and began praying that we would reach town safely.

A man standing near the driver commented to him, "White knuckle driving today, ould son. I don't envy you your job." Just then the bus rear slid sideways towards the path, and we were all pushed towards that side. There were a few screams from behind me.

The driver, with difficulty, got the bus back in a straight line, and we moved forward again.

"Bloody Corpo!" The driver's anger was evident. "Road gritting, how are ye! They shove out grit like it was sugar going into their tea, sparing like. They said they were out at seven this morning. They were in their arse!"

We slowly made the journey into town, and I called into the shop on Eden Quay as usual for the milk. Nellie came out from the counter smiling broadly, milk in hand.

"Happy Christmas, May!" she said, offering her cheek to be kissed. I returned the compliment. She then rummaged behind the counter. "Your Christmas biscuits," she said, and straightened up. I stood with mouth open in surprise. "Your biscuits," she said, "I told you. . ."

I'd expected a small round box of biscuits like those in the shop with a nice picture on the front. This was a big square box, wrapped up in Christmas paper and with twine forming a useful handle to carry it. I swallowed. "I thought. . ." Nellie laughed.

"Surprised?" That was Rosie come from the back room. "That's from Nellie and me, for the little ones, like." She handed me a box of toffees and a Christmas card. "There you go. Happy Christmas to you and yours, May." I bent down to kiss her cheek and responded to the good wishes. She held my head down for a moment. "No cutting down on your eating, May.

Promise me that." I muttered, "No, never," and thanked her and Nellie, my cheeks scarlet and eyes suddenly moist.

Jackie Mooney offered his services as carrier and took the biscuits off the counter to some ribald comments from his mates. He waited patiently at the office door while I fumbled for the key and then deposited the box in a corner neatly for me.

"Happy Christmas," he said, and took my hand in his and smiled. "See you in the New Year." Then he ran swiftly down the stairs.

I started to put away the things, then heard Terry's whistle down the corridor and went to the door to call him.

"Yes, m'm," he said, filling the pipe in the ritual I knew so well. "What can I do you for?"

"Last night, well, I can't understand it. First, the money for the hospital. Sure, it could only have been about twenty pounds, if that. It wouldn't have been worthwhile for the hospital. . ."

"So." Terry lit the tobacco with the blowtorch and puffed away, the smoke spiralling towards the ceiling. "But you don't know the full of it, girl. You see, 'Two-Gun' went to Johnny Weir, he's chairman of the Undertakers' Branch. It was their do in the Hotel Branch Hall. He told him the sob story, let down not only with the hall but also the acts, and no money to give the kids in the hospital a Christmas treat. Johnny reacted as Tom expected. It would be all right for him to make a bucket collection after the dinner, so three stalwarts did the job with the buckets. Just about every man jack in the hall gave a quid, some even more.

"The employers' group, when they heard what was going on, said they'd match the collection. So they doubled the stakes. Got quite a few bob." Terry began to poke at the pipe with a thing like a miniature poker.

"But. . ."

"The Undertakers' Ball, sure that's the best do of any here in the union. Best grub, free drink, good entertainment and great spot prizes. There's great crack between the mutes and the bosses. I suppose it stands to reason. For 364 days in the year they've got to look sad and dignified when they're working. God, if you get an invitation there you'd be made up." He turned to go.

"Terry, the little house and Santa going down the chimney, where did you get that?"

"You liked that, did you?" Terry chuckled. "Well, the tree would only fit there, and we couldn't have someone walking into the back of it. So Tom says," and Terry did a good imitation of Tom's voice, "'Terry, get something to block off that corridor, both ends, you understand. ASAP.'"

Terry chuckled. "Honest to God, sometimes you'd think they think I'm some sort of eejit or something. ASAP if you please."

"Terry. . ."

"Well, the bit of plywood was OK at your end. It wouldn't be seen."

"And you can't write in a straight line either," I interjected.

Terry grinned and began to rub more tobacco in the palm of his hand. "Well, I borrowed the cottage from the Abbey Theatre set dock, just out there in the lane. Joe Skerrett said, 'Well, you can have a castle wall, a manor house or a cottage,' so I chose the cottage. Seemed more in keeping with this kip. As for the Santa, well, I added that bit myself. Just a bit of plywood and a lick of paint and, of course, the artistic eye. But I thought, sure the kids might get a bit of a kick out of it. It's gone down to the hospital as the backdrop to the tree."

"Why was the front door locked? I thought Frances would kill you."

"I always get the blame! I told them, all them bleedin' experts, that if they used too much extra power, the fuses would go. So they'd lights, heat, electric boilers, a raft of things, all plugged in, and then they shove on the Christmas lights, and we're plunged into darkness. And where is the tree standing? You've got it in one. The fuses were right behind the Christmas tree. And what do the experts do? They say 'Do this,' 'Do that,' but they don't lift a finger themselves. And they'd no light and no screwdriver and no cop-on either. But could they leave me alone to get on with the job? Not on your life. Now the lack of chairs was a miscalculation. No access to passage or to offices, no chairs."

Terry laughed and ambled off, his pipe back in his pocket, and I couldn't help but smile to myself.

It was a strange day in the office. Members came in, were offered a drink or a cup of tea. Biscuits and chocolates were left open for whoever wanted to help themselves. I found myself mainly occupied in washing and drying cups and glasses and ensuring that the more diffident of our visitors got their share of the goodies that were going. Money came in and went out as people drew their commissions. There was shop talk and social chit-chat, rumours about what job was doing well or another that didn't look good. Both Jim and Sadie did their job as hosts, mingling in a convivial and friendly way, making sure that nobody was neglected.

At half-twelve Jim got into his coat and scarf, pulled on his gloves and took up his briefcase.

"I'll be away out to Blackrock, Sadie," he said, "so I'll leave you to hold the fort. Should be back about half-three with any luck. Now, May, I'll bring the car around to the door, so I'd appreciate it if you're ready to go in about five minutes. I can't linger there at the bus stop or I might get a bus making for my back bumper."

I made two trips with my things and stood, bags at my feet, in the doorway till I saw him pull in at the kerb. Bags pushed into the boot, Jim settled back to drive with care along the frosty roads to drop me off at the shops near my home.

"The main roads are OK now," he said, "but the side roads, well, that's another story. Sorry I can't give you a lift back, but I have to go the rounds in each of the factories I visit or someone gets insulted. And I have to drink more cups of tea than I care to think about."

When we got to the shops in my area, there was Con standing at the chipper a good deal cleaner and neater than the last time I saw him. I got out of the car and thanked Jim and introduced him to Con, then took my bags, Con taking the biscuits and hefting the weight, before taking another couple of bags.

"That and that bag are for hiding; the rest are OK for the house," I said as we carefully made our way down the by-road. The neighbour opposite us took in the surprise items that couldn't be brought home to peeping eyes.

"How's Paddy, Con?" I asked.

"He's sore, cuts and bruises; he can only hobble along. But he's on his feet and he's eating, and Larry says that's the main thing." Obviously Con had found a hero to be admired in Larry. "But the round now, that's a different thing. Jude thinks he can get a horse and maybe a milk cart, but it's more like a chariot really. He's moaning that it won't hold half the load, and that means he loses cash. I don't know what he plans about me. This would have to happen right when the Christmas tips should be rolling in."

As we walked down the road, Con seemed to have moved beyond the saga of Paddy's fall and was now fully into the snowball battle that loomed in the afternoon. Apparently it was a battle to the death between his age group in our street against a similar age group two streets away, with no quarter asked or given. He was full of plans and strategies. They had their cache of snowballs already made and hidden, and they'd a plan to lure their enemies down a particular pathway in the park, and then they'd "mow 'em down" with the ferocity of their attack.

I only had a few minutes to bolt down a sandwich with a cup of tea before making back for the bus, which, this time, made an unadventurous journey into town. Back in the office more people had arrived, and some of those I'd seen earlier were still there but decidedly the worse for wear.

Paddy McLoughlin put his head over my shoulder and surveyed the scene. "Same as ours," he commiserated. "Once they knock off work they work on the gargle. Ye'll be hard pressed to get rid of them by six. Jumbo'll have to do a 'Time, gentlemen, time' routine when he wants to get home."

He shuffled a bit and went a bit pink in the face, and then produced a little gift all wrapped in Christmas paper. "It's for you," he said gruffly, "for doing the Florence Nightingale act."

He then thrust the parcel into my hand and bent quickly and kissed my cheek with a muttered "Happy Christmas". With that he was gone clattering down the stairs.

I made my way through the crowd to my desk and put the parcel into a drawer, still in a state of shock. There were glasses and cups waiting to be washed, and I collected them and did the necessary. I then sat down to take in money from the recent arrivals. Suddenly I heard Eddie the chair call for silence and looked up from my tot to find all eyes focussed on me.

"On behalf of the branch and on my own behalf," Eddie said, looking at me directly, "it gives me great pleasure to give you this little gift, May. I hope when you use it it'll remind you of us and this great celebration we share together."

In a daze I went and was soundly kissed on both cheeks by Eddie to rather boisterous applause. Jim stood up and beckoned me forward. "I've carried this union badge in my pocket for the last few days waiting for the opportunity to give it to you, May. I think this is the opportune moment." He pinned the badge to my cardigan.

"You now wear the badge of your trade," he said with a smile. He then raised his glass. "To the newest recruit in the office," he said, "let's raise our glasses in toast."

Bee started to sing "For she's a jolly good fellow," which was enthusiastically taken up by those crammed around. That started the singsong they'd all been waiting for, and the singing went off at full gallop with Eddie acting as emcee.

When eventually I got back to my desk, it was to find Frances sitting on it chatting away to a group of people. She'd a new fur coat on, hair newly done, make-up expertly applied and wispy little sandals on her feet. When she saw me she gestured she'd meet me outside, and I made my way out as quickly as I could.

"Just wanted to say 'Happy Christmas'," she said. "I'm off now. Won't see you till after it's all over."

"Lovely coat," I ran my finger along the fur. "Going somewhere special?"

"Special? No, not really. There's a do in the Shelbourne, maybe a bit of a dance. But special, no, I couldn't say that."

She fumbled in the big leather handbag and produced a gift-wrapped parcel. "There, that's for you. No big deal. From the senior partner to the junior. Us young ones have got to stick together! Happy Christmas, May." With that she was gone, her high heels tip-tapping their way down the wooden stairs.

As I stood at the office door, Frank Robbins came along and unlocked his office door. "Have you got a minute, May?" he called.

I nodded and followed him into his office, and he rummaged around his desk drawer. "Something I thought you'd be interested in," he said. "If I can lay my hands on it." He drew out a picture and held it towards me. "It's the Countess in her Citizen Army uniform," he said. "Very different from the ball gown in the other formal portrait."

I looked over his shoulder. The photo was one of those old sepia prints. It showed a woman in a military uniform, with a hat with a cockade, pointing a revolver across a barricade in a very calm and determined fashion, eyes intent on what she was doing.

He put the photo into an envelope and then held a small piece of paper towards me. "This was written by Cecil Day Lewis. It's just a fragment of his poem but important to remember."

I read it slowly.

> "The road to Connolly and Stephen's Green
> Showed clear. The great heart which defied
> Irish prejudice, English snipers, died
> A little, not to have shared a grave with the fourteen.
> And when the Treaty emptied the British jails,
> A haggard woman returned
> And Dublin went wild to greet her.
> But still it was not enough: 'an iota
> Of compromise,' she cried, 'and the Cause fails.'
> Nest destroyed, eagles undone."

"I'm not into this Christmas gift business, May," Frank said, "but there's the Countess as she appeared to the British military in the Rising. And that poem gives some idea of how Dublin people felt about her."

I looked at him in complete surprise as he put the poem into the envelope with the photo and gave them to me.

When I got back to the office, the hooley was in full swing. Someone had produced a harmonica to aid the singing, and the place was crammed with people. Jim caught my eye. "I think you should make for home now, May," he said. "Can you get your things out of the press, and I'll get your coat from the inside office and meet you at the top of the stairs."

I did, with some difficulty, and he was waiting with my coat talking to a man. He held my coat and I got into it, astonished because nobody had done that since I was Kevin's age. "Now, have you got everything?" Jim asked, excusing himself for a moment from the man. "I'll see you out the door. That bus stop outside can be a bit boisterous at times."

As we went down the stairs, he asked how the do had gone the night before, but he obviously knew something about it already.

"You met Abina, I understand," he remarked. "One of the best, God knows. Her husband, Dinnie, was killed in that accident down on the docks. Another young lad was killed too, and Johnny Murphy broke his back. They were unloading a grain ship and the cargo shifted. That'd be four months before the last baby was born. The boys did their best for all three lads, but Abina just went back to trading, said she'd manage OK. One independent lady."

I was astonished. "She sings so well and loves music," I offered. "You'd think. . ."

"She has no heart for show business stuff," Jim said. In the hallway he took a little parcel out of his pocket and handed it to me.

"A little like bringing coals to Newcastle," he laughed. "Just a little gift, a pen actually, because I believe a good pen is essential to a good writer."

He put his hand into his jacket pocket. "And this, well, it's a gift given to me. I prefer not to have too much spirits lying around the house, so I thought it'd maybe help your father ease down. Just a little drop in hot water with a bit of sugar and a few cloves can take some of the misery out of your bones when you're a bit down."

He put a hip-flask sized bottle of Jameson into my bag, bent quickly and kissed my cheek and wished me "Happy Christmas". While I was still responding, he'd the door open, had checked the lay-out outside, and when I stumbled out, shut the door quickly with a smile and a wave of his hand.

Town was packed with shoppers, nearly everybody carrying odd-shaped parcels. One man, dressed very formally in a black overcoat, white silk scarf and trousers with a stripe, was pushing a doll's pram, complete with flaxen-haired doll, along the path.

"She your first?" a wag asked, and his companions nearly burst a gut laughing, but the man never even smiled.

The bus, full at first, emptied out most shoppers at Grafton Street, leaving a bit more space to stretch. I'd my bag on my knee with the presents, my mind on what might be in them, when I heard the singers at the back of the bus.

There were three men, all jarred out of their minds, and presumably what they were singing made some sense to them. For the listener, however, the only discernable words (or indeed tune) was when they together shouted, "Fine girl you are!"

The long-suffering conductor, standing balanced against one of the metal poles as he negotiated change for a customer, shouted back to them. "Would you ever have a bit of order down there in the back of the bus! Now, a bit of order, if you please!"

There was a blessed silence for a moment. Then "Don't mind if I do," one of the men shouted back. "That's three double whiskeys and three chasers! That's our order!" They thought this hilariously funny and were still repeating the tag line as I got off the bus.

I picked my way carefully initially, but realising that there was nobody about, then childishly stamped on the iced puddles to see the ice fragment into star shapes. There was a choice then, down the broader, more open avenue, or a short cut by the back lane. Just at the moment of decision I hesitated.

My father was plodding along the avenue, head down, hands in his pockets. For one moment my instinct was to take the short cut, to avoid trying to get over the gulf that lay between us. The thought appalled me. It seemed so disloyal. Then I was running down the avenue regardless of a possible slip and shouting, "Da, Da, wait for me." He turned around and stopped, and as I reached him, breathless, I wondered what on earth to say.

"It's yourself," he observed mildly. "Aren't you home early?"

"Yes, there was a bit of a boozing session in the office, so Jim sent me home early. And I'm finished work till after Christmas." I could have bit my tongue when I realised how that remark could appear to be a cut at him.

"M'm. So you're finished till after the holidays. I'm finished full stop," he said with some bitterness. "Paid off today. The young fellas will do Christmas Eve; the work is light and there'll be a few jars stirring wherever they go. So us oldies got the chop."

I didn't know what to say but got stuck into recounting the story of the jarred group on the bus and their rejoinder to the conductor, then into the soberly dressed man nonchalantly pushing a doll's pram through the crowds in town and what the young fellow had said. We walked along together, but in our minds still remained far apart. Then his hand came out and took my bag to carry.

"What have you here," he asked, "the Crown jewels?"

"Just a few things I was given," I answered. "God, I was mortified." And I told him the story of having to go up and be presented with something by Eddie with everyone clapping.

"What is it?" he asked.

"I don't know. I'm leaving opening it till Christmas morning, you know, like always." From the time I could remember we'd always done that in our house, opened any presents we got on Christmas morning. It had something to do with the day that was in it, being all together, sharing, being a family, but I couldn't put it into words.

"Still a baby?" he laughed. "Even at fifteen."

But his hand came out and took mine, and we walked together, stride for stride, the rest of the way down the avenue.

When I opened the door it was to a very peaceful domestic scene. My father had delayed to talk to a neighbour about a sick dog, so I went in alone. My mother was winding the wool Abbie held in a skein on her wrists, and they were chatting away amicably. Kate and Kevin sat in a corner busily engaged in drawing up their Christmas letter to Santa. At least Kate was doing the writing on a piece of cardboard. Kevin was drawing what, to him, was obviously a train with a wisp of smoke coming from the engine but to the rest of us would look just like a scribble. Con was busy with some engineering feat, which involved measuring with a knotted bit of twine and doing diagrams and calculations on a bit of paper.

"Da's right behind me," I said. "God, it's good to see you, Abbie. How are you?"

"This is an oasis of peace," Abbie said. "Sure, I don't know myself being a lady of leisure."

I kissed her cheek and went off to hang up my coat. In truth, Abbie looked anything but well. The twins that were now a reality seemed to be draining her strength. She seemed to be getting smaller, more worn, as the belly bump got bigger.

My mother handed me the ball of wool. "Would you carry on, May, while I look after your father? Honest to God, I got so involved in the chat with Abbie I clean forgot he'd be back early today." She disappeared into the back kitchen.

My father came in, bent and kissed Abbie's cheek, and welcomed her into his home, being quite charming. Then he excused himself to get washed and changed.

I started winding the wool and chatting with Abbie, but at the same time I was thinking maybe it'd be a good thing to give my father the slippers now rather than hold them back. I knew in my heart he'd never sit down with us in front of the range in his stocking feet with Abbie there. That, in his book, would be impolite. But we always. . .

I excused myself to Abbie and went over to Con. Looking over his shoulder, I saw he was transforming the sledge into a trolley. The measuring and the diagrams were trying to work out where the axles would go and how the front wheels could be steered. I hunkered down beside him.

"Con, I'm wondering if we should give Da the slippers now. He's finished in the post and his walking is done. I know it's not exactly Christmas. . ."

"But. . ." I could see the thoughts run through Con's mind, "he'd go to bed. Miss the Santa letters. Yes. I'll go get them."

He went off over the street to get the parcel and returned and handed it to me, still breathless. "But you do the giving," he said with a laugh. "You're the elder!"

I took the gaily wrapped present under the watchful eye of Abbie and went into the back kitchen. My mother was lancing a large blister on the sole of my father's foot, the antiseptic, the cotton wool, the plasters and the methylated bottle all at her elbow.

"Ah, May, give us a minute, please. This is not. . ."

"It's our Christmas gift, Da, for you. We thought slippers might help, be easier than boots. I know it's not the day for presents, but we thought maybe. . ."

I stopped, suddenly mute, and thrust the box towards him, tears not far away. "We just thought. . ."

He took the box and suddenly his arms were around me. "That's a lovely present. I never expected anything. But you shouldn't have done it. You need so many things, and I can't give them to you."

For a moment we stayed as we were, my mother still with the needle in her hand and the water in the basin growing cold.

"That's a lovely thought, child," she said, and wiped her eye with the back of her hand. "Now, go out and entertain Abbie. She'll be wondering what on earth we're up to."

I went back out, my eyes still moist, and took up the ball of wool. Con caught my eye and winked, and suddenly I knew in my heart that Christmas was going to be all right.

We had our tea wedged in a tight group around the table, Abbie in my father's chair, Kevin on Da's knee, Kate on mine, the rest elbow to elbow, enjoying a plate of my mother's stew, followed by apple pie, then tea and bread and jam for anyone who still had a gap to fill. Con retold the saga of Paddy's fall. Ger told about the bus that had got stuck on the Embankment with the passengers having to be rescued by the army. I told of my day, getting up to show the picture and the poem Frank Robbins had given me about Madame.

Abbie looked at it with interest. "My granny was in Cumann na mBan, the women's version of the Citizen Army," she said. "She used to talk yards about Madame. She called my mother Constance after her. I was nearly getting named Constance too," she laughed.

"And what happened?" I was curious.

"My mother had a yen after the books, you know, like Mills and Boon. All the heroines were called Cynthia and Octavia and things like that. I suppose I was lucky to get Abigail. It could have been worse."

I told them all about Abina and the concert and how enjoyable it had been.

"Have you been admiring my feet?" my father asked Abbie. "I'm wearing my first Christmas present, what do you think of that?" He held up his foot for all to admire, and Con gave me a thumbs up across the table.

His slippers having been duly admired, we cleared away the things to get down to the business of the Santa letters. That involved my mother using the damper to get the range set just right to ensure that the little one's letters went straight up the chimney right into the great one's hands.

My father, in the meantime, had Kate on his knee to ensure the letters were as clear as could be so that Santa knew exactly what to bring. Then they were cast into the red fire with great ceremony and, with the help of the adjustments my mother had made, went straight up the chimney as we all applauded.

Kate was prevailed upon to sing one of the carols from school, and she sang "Away in a Manger", and when she was applauded went on with "Adeste Fideles" in which we all joined. Kevin, not to be outdone, sang "Twinkle, Twinkle, Little Star", with a few prompts from my mother. Abbie sang "Once in Royal David's City". My father then ended the little recital with "Panis Angelicus", sounding very much like John McCormack. We then called it a day as Kevin's eyes shut of their own accord.

The little ones in bed, Josie and some of her family called to take Abbie home in the wheelchair, warmly wrapped up and very grateful for the session in peace and quiet. Eileen and Josie were a bit apprehensive of how she'd react when she saw what they'd done to her room in her absence.

"I think Josie's taste is in her arse," Eileen confided to me. "There's big roses plastered all over the wall, and the place still reeks of paint. Maybe it's better than it was. Anyway. I only hope Ma doesn't spot the bit that somehow got put on upside down."

We huddled around the dwindling heat of the range and talked about our plans for tomorrow and the big day to follow. Ger said his visits to the hospital had made him realise that money wasn't everything and what we had a lot of people would envy. My father looked a bit askance at that. "Money feeds a family," he said shortly.

"We'll manage," Con said. "You'll see, after Christmas things will look up. What we've got to do is to make sure the little ones get the best Christmas we can give them. Something they'll remember always, the magic that is Christmas, something money alone can't buy. After all, you gave it to us when we were kids, and I'm sure times weren't easy then either."

My mother looked at my father. "Do you remember our first Christmas? When we hadn't even a pot to boil the pudding? And yet we managed."

"And that was the nicest Christmas pudding I ever tasted," he laughed. "Now it's bedtime, a busy day tomorrow."

Before he turned off the light, my father went to the front door to check everything was OK. "Frost is going," he said, his eye on the sky. "Turn to sleet during the night, if I'm any judge of the weather." And with that, we all went off to bed.

CHAPTER TWENTY-THREE

NEXT MORNING I was awake early. Outside the drip-drip of the rain off the gutter verified my father's forecast. Indeed, as I looked out the window there was nothing to be seen but the sleety rain slanting up the cold grey street.

In the kitchen my mother was buttoning Eileen into her plastic coat against her protestations.

"You'd get your end of a cold without it, child," she remonstrated, pulling up the hood. "You have to have some protection."

"I feel like a cod in a pot," Eileen complained, the coat barely fitting over her ordinary coat. "Oh, all right," she conceded. "I have to go. That ould go-by-the-wall Mr Parker will be counting the seconds I'm late in opening up."

I caught her at the door. "What did your ma think of the decoration?" I asked. "Was she pleased?"

"She nearly passed out when the roses hit her for a start," Eileen said. "But give my ma her due, she never said anything about the upside-down bit, even though her eye kept being drawn back to it. I think the smell of the paint made her a bit sick. At least I hope it's that. See you later."

It was going to be a busy day for us. My father drew a bucket of potatoes from his cache in the shed, cleaned them out and left them ready for next day. He used his bike to call to a plot-mate for a few mixed veggies. I saw Con turning up his nose at the turnips and parsnips he brought in. Con himself went for the bread to the bakery and came back with two bags full, including a good selection of fancies. My mother collected her piece of roast beef from the butcher, pleased that she got a good bit of suet and a few bones that would make good soup.

In the meantime I was wading through the ironing, to make sure we'd all be spick and span for the big day itself. Ger was on duty till two and then would go down to his newsagent friend for the final round-up of orders.

"Always at the last minute somebody's cocked up: an order forgotten, mislaid, a young fellow doesn't turn up, a snotty ould customer who's got to be placated. They never forget; anyone who has anything goes wrong at Christmas has a memory like an elephant."

Then there was the washing bit. The big galvanised bath would be doing Trojan duty today. And confession too. All of us adults, except my father, would be going to one of the sessions. For some undisclosed reason my father exempted himself from that particular chore.

Midnight mass was something too he missed. There the reason was that someone had to stay home with the little ones. He'd go to mid-day mass and stroll to the church and back to "get a bit of air" on his own.

But at five o'clock today there was a most important chore he had to fulfil for Kate and Kevin. On Radio Éireann a programme would be heard covering Santa's departure from Lapland on his sleigh with the reindeer pulling it, crammed with parcels for good kids all around the world. My father would sit with the two young kids who were delirious with excitement, just as we used to be, and reinforce the magic the programme evoked for young listeners.

For the rest of the evening, mind you, we'd be asked from time to time, "Is Santa across America yet?" or "Has he been to Rome?" as the map my father drew of the projected journey was creased and uncreased by eager little hands.

Then there was the visit to Abbie and our next-door neighbours, and, in the evening, my mother made the red jelly that Kevin loved, made custard and boiled the little pudding her sister had given her.

After tea, all meals being a bit haphazard as they were fitted into the day's programme, we had the ceremony of placing the little Baby Jesus in the crib, Kevin doing the honours aided by Kate. The final touch was the lighting of the red candle in its holly bedecked saucer in the window by Kate. Then bedtime for the little ones, with one final look out the door in case they could see Santa's sleigh flying over the houses opposite.

Then Con went around to Jackie's for the cot. I went over to our neighbours for the secret parcels, my mother and father diplomatically retired to the back kitchen, and we started the assembly line.

There was Kate's doll, resplendent in her woolly matinee jacket and dress, bonnet atop her sculpted hairdo, sitting in her pink cot against a lace-edged pillow, covered by a pink rosy bedspread. The rest of her alternative wardrobe was contained in a transparent plastic envelope: her coat, bootees, vest, panties and bonnet. Beside it stood the little teaset covered in Christmas paper and glittery tinsel with Kate's name on it. Hung over it her little cotton drawstring bag with her name sewn on filled with small things: chocolate, fruit, sweets, silvery money in a little net bag and a paper doll with her assorted wardrobe.

Kevin's bag had almost exactly the same things. They always had to be equal. Beside it stood the Black Bob book and the box of cowboys and Indians all done up in Christmas paper.

Beside it I placed my mother's present and my father's cigarettes, then Con's knife, and a colourful tie for Ger. Ger put in a little parcel with my name on it. Could it be a diary, I wondered. I'd have to wait to see. I put down the presents I'd got in Liberty Hall, and we sat back on our heels and admired the set-up.

My mother and father came back in with a little box each, probably sweets, soft parcels for Ger and Con, which proved to be a hand-knitted scarf and gloves respectively. When she handed me mine I couldn't believe it! It had to be, by the shape of it, a handbag. I looked at her in total surprise.

"The best I could do," she murmured. "I hope you like it." I was mute. I couldn't say anything. Then she put down a selection box beside each of the kid's presents. "There, that's it, I think."

The bell rang for midnight mass and we made a hurried departure, leaving my father to keep the fire stoked up and to have a cup of tea ready when we got back.

As we walked around to the church, a small section of many small groups, I remembered the Mayo man and what he'd said about walking the black road and the sound of the lullaby coming back from the stones, as people, those seen and unseen, added their voices in the praise of the infant Jesus.

CHAPTER TWENTY-FOUR

W E WERE PART of the army of people coming home from midnight mass, with the peals of our church bells, punctuated by the tinny little voice of the Poor Clare's convent, answering the bells all around that proclaimed the saviour had been born.

Eileen and I walked together. "Do you think it's a bit much, May, the way they gloss over the actual birth?" Eileen asked me.

I gaped at her in absolute astonishment. "What. . . I mean, I don't understand. . ."

"Well, the angel came to Mary and told her about the conception and all that. Joseph didn't have much gumption, did he? I mean, all that Bethlehem business and the stable and all. You'd think he'd have taken more care of her. And there's never any talk about what she went through in the birth and all that. Suddenly the child is there, like as though it was born without suffering or anything. And them priests, sure what would they know about childbirth?"

"Yes, I see what you mean. You're worried about your ma, aren't you?"

"I am, I really am. She's not well at all. Mrs Jennings says one of the babies isn't thriving. If it dies me ma would have to carry it right through till the other baby is born. Imagine that, May, a dead baby inside you. And not a damn thing you can do about it."

The grip Eileen had on my arm hurt and I gently released it. "But the hospital. . ."

"She's a nine-day wonder in the hospital. But does anyone ever ask her how she feels, what's inside her mind? She's scared, May. My ma, for the first time I've ever known it, is scared. She's afraid for the babies and for herself too, and us. As for me da! 'You'll be up and as good as new in no time,' that's all he says, and then goes up to the pub or the bookies where he doesn't have to see her fight for her breath."

"I didn't know. . . She seemed in good form yesterday."

"She didn't even fight about the wallpaper, May. If she was in form she'd tear strips off us for the way we did that room yesterday, but she was too tired to fight." Eileen held the tears back with difficulty.

"What can we do? Maybe try to keep her spirits up till she's back in the hospital. Probably that's the best we can do." I knew it was cold comfort.

"I'll go home tonight, May," Eileen said. "It wouldn't be Christmas really unless I woke up at home. Even if I can't do much for her, at least I'd be there to keep the kids in order. You see, the little ones don't know anything is wrong, and they keep vying for her attention. And she tries. . ."

Clumsily we hugged, whispered our Christmas greetings, then she was gone.

At home, things were a great deal more cheerful. My father had kept the fire up and had tea and toast ready for us. We sat down comfortably, with comments about the ceremony, the singing, the new clothes sported by some neighbours and the do-up of the Church for the festive occasion.

I looked at the Santa spread of goodies carefully laid out in the corner and wondered at the back of my mind what was in my parcels. There was the pen and what I was sure was a handbag, but the others. . .

My mother brought my father a glass with a hot amber liquid in it. "A hot whiskey," she said. "May's boss recommended it. Good for aching bones, he said. So down that, my good man."

She raised her cup of tea in a toast. "Happy Christmas to all here and all our friends."

Bemused, he took the glass, raised it in toast to her and responded, "Happy Christmas, Peg, and many of them."

We all echoed the Christmas wishes and then took to our beds, conscious that it wouldn't be many hours before Kate and Kevin would be creeping down to the kitchen to see if Santa had got their Christmas letter and left what they wanted in his long trek right across the globe.

Indeed, it seemed that my head had only hit the pillow when Kate pulled on my shoulder. "May, May, I think he's been. Come down and see what he's brought!"

Tousled, red-eyed, clad in bits and pieces of clothes, my father still unshaven, we gathered in the kitchen where the fire was a mass of grey ashes and it was cold.

"First things first," my father said. "The fire first and a few clothes on. It's too cold to be standing around."

He and Ger looked after the fire. My mother got the excited chattering kids into the warmest clothes she could find. Con and I put the kettle on and set the table for breakfast.

"Now," my father said, "let's see what the good man has left for you."

We all gathered around, my mother with a mug of pale tea in her hand.

Kate sat on her hunkers, her mouth wide open, as she looked at her doll with total wonder. "She's really for me, is she?"

My mother nodded. "And she has her own cot and a change of clothes and all. Isn't she the lucky doll? What'll you call her?"

"Daisy," Kate said immediately. "Daisy O'Brien. I think that's a nice name. Can I hold her?" My mother took the doll out of the cot and put it in her arms.

"Isn't Santa the decent man all the same," my father said. "And what has he left the little man?" He took out the Black Bob book and handed it to Kevin sitting on his knee, thumb sucking vigorously.

"Do you want to open it?"

"You," Kevin said. "You do it."

My father took the Christmas paper off, carefully putting it away to be used again, and the book was revealed in all its glory.

"That's for you," my father said. "Santa left it, isn't he the kind man. Look at all the stories that's there to be read."

He opened the book, showing Kevin the pictures. As Kevin's confidence grew he started to identify things, cows, sheep, pigs and so on, all with the sheep dog hero showing his prowess in resolving the most dangerous of situations by his cleverness.

"And that?" Kate pointed. "Is that for me too?"

My mother nodded. Kate opened the parcel, carefully laying aside the paper in imitation of her father. "Look, it's a little teaset. Will you look at the size of it?" She counted the cups and saucers. "Six of each, and a jug, and a sugar bowl. Ah, look at the little teapot. Isn't it a little dote!"

Then it was Kevin's turn. The box of cowboys and Indians left him speechless. Ger lined them out on the lino in front of the range, and the Indian chief with the war feathers on the pinto pony did look impressive, as Ger had said.

My father said, "Breakfast now before we go any further. Now, come on, Kevin, Kate, up on the bench and a bowl of porridge and a slice or two of bread."

Reluctantly they clambered up, with wistful eyes turned back to the little cotton bags.

Con lingered. "I think I see my name on something here," he said offhandedly. "Can I have a look?"

Ger and I looked at each other.

"Bring it with you," my father said. Con had his porridge and a couple of slices of bread and jam and a mug of tea, with the parcel beside his plate, his eyes on it appraisingly. "Go on, open it," my father gave way. Con did so and sat transfixed, his mouth in a big '"O" of astonishment. "It's a knife," he said when he got his breath back. "A knife with all the gadgets." He began to open them one by one. "I don't believe it!" He looked at it again. "But how. . .?"

"Santa," my mother said with a warning look. "Santa's a decent man all the same."

After breakfast the little ones concentrated on their little bags, which we used in place of stockings, and my mother laid down the law about what could be eaten and what must be left aside. Our presents were small, my mother's blouse, my father's cigarettes, Ger's scarf and garish tie, and Con's gloves. For me specifically, my handbag, Jim's pen in its own case, Frances's little manicure set, the branch's stationery set, Ger's little diary and Paddy Mcloughlin's box of embroidered handkerchiefs.

"Well now," my father sat back in his chair by the range. "Maybe a walk for the little ones would be in order before their dinner." He looked at me.

"To see the crib," the little ones said together. "Oh yes, the crib. We want to see the crib."

Again, this was something of a family ritual. The crib was in a shed in the grounds of the Carmelite monastery. Somehow it seemed a very appropriate setting. The shed was low and dark, smelling of dampness and the straw that covered the floor. The figures were, I suppose, half life size, well lit, with only a kneeler between us and the well-known scene. The kids looked at it with something of awe. I had two dominant thoughts. One was to make sure Kevin didn't pick up the baby and try to bring it home as he'd done last year. That'd been funny in one way, exasperating in another. To him at three years of age, the baby shouldn't be left there with these other cold statues, and he'd wanted to take him home to take care of him. I'd been mortified, but the brother who'd appeared had stifled a smile and said Kevin had the right instincts.

But the other thought was what Eileen had said about her mother. It tied in with my own strengthening feeling that somehow women were treated as belonging to a lower caste, as though they didn't have fears, feelings and dreams that had importance for society generally. That what they felt didn't matter.

Ger would laugh at me for that bit about society. Why worry about society, he'd say, society never worried its head about us. But was that enough?

My thoughts were stopped in their tracks. "Kevin, you can't have the baby, come out of there." His little figure was squeezing determinedly under the edge of the kneeler, concentrating on grabbing the infant from its manger. I caught him firmly by the back of his coat.

"You can't have it. The baby has to stay here with its mother."

"Let him hold it a moment," a voice behind me said. "He's got the right instincts." It was the same brother as had appeared last year.

"I got a doll from Santa," Kate said firmly. "He thinks that's his. But it's not a doll."

Reluctantly Kevin relinquished his hold, and the brother put the baby back in position. "We'll say a little prayer now for the baby and its mother," the brother said benignly.

Kevin didn't understand that, but realising that something was required of him he sang his party piece, "Twinkle, Twinkle, Little Star."

The brother beamed. "Very appropriate. You've got a grand little lad there."

I hurriedly pulled both kids out and said my goodbyes before Kate added some of the less appropriate words she'd learnt in school to ease the burden and the boredom of praying.

At home things were in festive swing. The table was set with the best we had. There was the smell of roasting meat and a roaring fire in the range, with my mother presiding over steaming pots in the back kitchen. My father sat smoking a cigarette, a glass at his elbow, and wearing his slippers while he read Kevin's book.

"You know, that's the cleverest dog, that Black Bob," he said to Kevin. "Maybe we'll have a go at reading a bit tonight."

Kevin beamed with happiness, and I refrained from telling about the baby, and to my surprise Kate did too.

The dinner was grand. We all were agreed on that. My father had even somehow procured a few crackers and balloons, which added greatly to the festive occasion.

Sitting around the fire later, my father read the first chapter of Kevin's new book. Kate cuddled Daisy on her knee and fed her from her little teaset. Con tried out his knife on a few bits of wood. Ger and I did a jigsaw, and my mother knitted up the wool she and Abbie had wound together. There was peace, happiness and contentment in the room with us that night, despite all the problems that lurked outside.

Later my mother stood at the door looking out into the night, the Christmas candle flickering behind her echoing those in the windows around us. She looked back at us with her usual smile.

"Sure, God is good all the same," she said quietly.

"And the devil's not such a bad fellow," we responded as one, grinning at the stupidity of the old tag.

"Anyone for a cup of tea?" she asked. "And there's still a bit of pudding left if you're interested."

I thought then about how my life had changed in the three months or so I'd been working in the union. I'd gone to work as an impressionable young one directly from school, and I'd learned so much from Jim and Terry, Paddy and Tommy, Nellie and Rosie, "Two-Gun" O'Reilly, Jackie, Golly and all the others.

Maybe with the help of those union people, society could be made to change, be made to take responsibility for those less well off, those who clung to life itself by their very fingertips, always on the verge of falling into the pit.

EPILOGUE

TO ENSURE THAT none of my family or neighbours suffers embarrassment or hurt by events depicted by me, I have not used their real names. My intention was to show by a process of reminiscences what was a fairly standard working-class lifestyle with all its grimness, particularly for women, in the late 1940s.

To fit the timeframe of the book, I have also moved away from a calendar timescale.

My depiction of what it was like to work in the old Liberty Hall has to be seen through the eyes of a young school leaver who saw things without understanding what she saw in many cases.

I have some reservations about using actual names of people in this situation and inventing dialogue for them. But to give them pseudonyms, I believe, would do them a disservice since their contribution to Irish life and the Irish Trade Union movement at that period needs to be recorded. In extenuation of what I've done, I can only say how much affection I feel for so many of the people I met in the old Liberty Hall and how much they influenced my thinking.

That period of 1947 was the worst period for my family. Shortly afterwards, my father got a permanent job as a chauffeur where he was quite happy working until his death. My mother lived to the ripe old age of ninety-two and saw her children settle in "good, steady" jobs: Ger in Guinness, Con in Bus Éireann, Kate in the ITGWU and Kevin in the Gas Company.

Abbie lived to celebrate her ninetieth birthday in great style, surrounded by her children, grandchildren and great-grandchildren. She remained the same woman of courage, a survivor in a period that was exceedingly hard on women such as Abbie. At her party she held her latest great-grandchild in her arms. "God, I do love the feel of a new baby."

For myself, those first few months working in old Liberty Hall were the forerunner of forty-five happy years working first for the ITGWU, and later for SIPTU, when the amalgamation of the two unions undid the split of the 1920s.

Having started in the clerical grade, I followed Frances Lambert into the industrial area, where we were the only two women staff members in that full-time grade at that time. When the union set up an equality unit in 1982, I was appointed as women's affairs official and so was enabled to deal directly with the problems for women I had identified in my own life so many years earlier.

LILY O'CONNOR

Can Lily O'Shea Come Out to Play?

A bestseller in Ireland and Australia, a fascinating story of growing up Protestant in Dublin.

This vivid memoir of a childhood in the 1930s and '40s is marked by its narrator's consciousness of her status as an outsider, for Lily is a child of a mixed marriage, baptised a Protestant but living in a Catholic community. The originality of this account of a working-class childhood is its portrait of a spirited girl coming to terms with her difference. At its heart this is a universal story of childhood; of hardship and joy, of violence, poverty, pleasure, humour and, over all, humanity.

"Anyone with half an interest in times gone by will enjoy this well-written anecdotal book." *Irish Criticism*

"A vibrant recollection of childhood, this – honest, warm and often moving." *Examiner*

ISBN 0 86322 267 6; Paperback

ROSEMARY CONRY
Flowers of the Fairest

"Has the ring of authenticity. This is a book to be recommended. . .
Surprisingly, the story is told with much humour." *Irish Independent*

"A fascinating first-hand account of one child's experience of TB in the
1940s. It is full of interesting details of the little everyday routines of life
on a veranda, with all its pain and its fun. . . A lovely book that gives us a
fascinating insight into a world that thankfully we will never know."
Books Ireland

ISBN 0 86322 303 6; Paperback

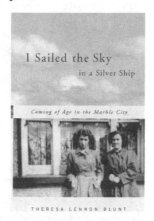

THERESA LENNON BLUNT
I Sailed the Sky in a Silver Ship

"Much more than a chronicle of life in Ireland, it is the story of a girl
desperate to escape the misery and embarrassment . . . The author's
descriptive powers vividly evoke her time and place, and she has
succeeded in relating her tale of a turbulent childhood and youth with
little trace of self-pity." *BookView Ireland*

"From the opening passages of the book the reader is swept back in time
and place through the author's descriptive powers, rich narrative, and
exquisite use of metaphor." *The Harp*

ISBN 0 86322 304 4; Paperback

WILSON JOHN HAIRE
The Yard

"This riproaring yarn about a lad plucked from a rural Belfast environment and plonked into the Harland & Wolff shipyard as an office boy has enough meat in it to service perhaps a dozen books of memoirs, but the author, whose thinly-disguised autobiography it is, has compressed them all into a smorgasbord of earthy irreverence, hardnosed stoicism and some of the most ribtickling anecdotes we've heard this side of Frank McCourt." *Books Ireland*

ISBN 0 86322 296 X; Paperback

JOHN B. KEANE
The Bodhrán Makers

The first and best novel from one of Ireland's best-loved writers, a moving and telling portrayal of a rural community in the '50s, a poverty-stricken people who never lost their dignity.

"Furious, raging, passionate and very, very funny." *Boston Globe*

"This powerful and poignant novel provides John B. Keane with a passport to the highest levels of Irish literature." *Irish Press*

"Sly, funny, heart-rending. . . Keane writes lyrically; recommended." *Library Journal*

ISBN 0 86322 300 1; Paperback

KITTY FITZGERALD

"Mystery and politics, a forbidden sexual attraction that turns into romance; Kitty Fitzgerald takes the reader on a gripping roller coaster through the recent past. In *Small Acts of Treachery* a woman of courage defies the power not only of the secret state but of sinister global elites. This is a story you can't stop reading, with an undertow which will give you cause to reflect." Sheila Rowbotham

"[*Small Acts of Treachery*] is a super book with a fascinating story and great characters. The book is all the more impressive because of the very sinister feeling I was left with that it is all too frighteningly possible." *Books Ireland*

ISBN 086322 297 8; Paperback

"*Snapdragons* is a rattling one-sit read, rich with Irish rhythms and laced with a wonderfully bitter and witty ongoing dialogue between the heroine Bernice and her cantankerous, wheedling God. The early, Irish part of the novel is a powerful evocation of a godfearing rural community which reveals itself to be every bit as cruel as the seedy Birmingham underworld to which the girls escape." *Northern Review*

"Startling, humorous, light of touch." *Books Ireland*

ISBN 0 86322 258 7; Paperback

MARY ROSE CALLAGHAN
The Visitors' Book

"Callaghan takes the romantic visions some Americans have of Ireland and dismantles them with great comic effect. . . It is near impossible not to find some enjoyment in this book, due to the fully-formed character of Peggy who, with her contrasting vulnerability and searing sarcasm, commands and exerts an irresistible charm." *Sunday Tribune*

ISBN 0 86322 280 3; Paperback

MARIE McGANN
The Drawbridge

"Marie McGann is a real find. She writes with the exhilaration and defiance of youth and the wisdom of age. A moving and triumphant novel." *Fay Weldon*

"An assured debut . . . At its heart [it] is about love in its many forms, and the struggle to throw off the shackles of defensiveness and self preservation and at last attain the freedom to love without fear." *Sunday Tribune*

ISBN 0 86322 271 4; Paperback